AA
NB

DETROIT PUBLIC LIBRARY

3 5674 04935786 7

D1034174

CHASE BRANCH LIBRARY
17731 W. SEVEN MILE RD.
DETROIT, MI 48235
578-8002

JUN 09

CH

THE PRINCIPLES AND
BENEFITS
OF
CHANGE

FULFILLING YOUR PURPOSE IN UNSETTLED TIMES

DR. MYLES MUNROE

WHITAKER
HOUSE

Unless otherwise indicated, Scripture quotations are taken from the *Holy Bible, New International Version*®, NIV®, © 1973, 1978, 1984 by the International Bible Society. Used by permission of Zondervan. All rights reserved. Scripture quotations marked (KJV) are taken from the King James Version of the Holy Bible. Scripture quotations marked (NKJV) are taken from the *New King James Version*, © 1979, 1980, 1982, 1984 by Thomas Nelson, Inc. Used by permission. Scripture quotations marked (NASB) are taken from the updated *New American Standard Bible*®, NASB®, © 1960, 1962, 1963, 1968, 1971, 1972, 1973, 1975, 1977, 1995 by The Lockman Foundation. Used by permission. (www.Lockman.org)

Some definitions of Hebrew and Greek words are taken from *Strong's Exhaustive Concordance* or the *New American Standard Exhaustive Concordance of the Bible* (NASC). The Lockman Foundation. Used by permission.

THE PRINCIPLES AND BENEFITS OF CHANGE:
Fulfilling Your Purpose in Unsettled Times
Hardcover edition

Dr. Myles Munroe
Bahamas Faith Ministries International
P.O. Box N9583
Nassau, Bahamas
bfmadmin@bfmmm.com
www.bfmmm.com; www.bfmi.tv; www.mylesmunroe.tv

ISBN: 978-1-60374-097-5
Printed in the United States of America
© 2009 by Dr. Myles Munroe

Whitaker House
1030 Hunt Valley Circle
New Kensington, PA 15068
www.whitakerhouse.com

Library of Congress Cataloging-in-Publication Data

Munroe, Myles.

The principles and benefits of change / Myles Munroe.

p. cm.

Summary: "Reveals how we can respond positively rather than react negatively to change that happens to us, around us, and within us and how we can initiate change, enabling us to fulfill our God-given purposes"—Provided by publisher.

ISBN 978-1-60374-097-5 (trade hardcover : alk. paper)   1. Change—Religious aspects—Christianity. I. Title.

BV4509.5.M86 2009

248.4—dc22

2009018191

No part of this book may be reproduced or transmitted in any form or by any means, electronic or mechanical—including photocopying, recording, or by any information storage and retrieval system—without permission in writing from the publisher. Please direct your inquiries to permissionseditor@whitakerhouse.com.

1 2 3 4 5 6 7 8 9 10 11 12 **W** 17 16 15 14 13 12 11 10 09

DEDICATION

To Ruth!

You have weathered the changes of my life for thirty years and taught me the value of the beauty of change.

To Charisa and Chairo!

I watched you successfully manage the changes from birth to adulthood, and I am proud of you. You taught me many of the principles in this work, and I trust you will maximize the changes throughout your lives.

To the over six billion planet dwellers on an earth that changes every minute. May this work equip you with the tools to not just watch things change but make things change for the better.

Acknowledgments

Since this book has been over twenty years in the making, I hope that all the leaders, friends, family members, and colleagues who have inspired me over the years will know my gratitude, even if there are too many to name on this page.

First and foremost, my thanks to my beloved wife, Ruth, who has stood by me and encouraged me to keep sharing my thoughts with the world.

Second, to my children, Charisa and Myles (Chairo) Munroe! Thank you for allowing me to fulfill my passions without a sense of guilt. Your patience and understanding are inspiring.

To my very talented, wise, and excellent editor, Lois Puglisi! Your commitment to perfection and quality is exceptional, and I owe you a deep sense of gratitude and appreciation for helping me deliver this work to the market of humanity. A philosopher is only as valuable as his readers; therefore, I thank you for helping this work make it to the hearts of men and women whom I hope will benefit from the content of these pages and make change a friend.

CONTENTS

PREFACE

Nothing is as permanent as change. Understanding this paradoxical truth transformed my life. It protected me when I was a youth, and it has helped guide me as an adult.

Change is natural to existence and common to all creation. Everything is in a constant state of change, and nothing can stop it. Change is both evidence that we are alive and proof that we are finite—because everything has its own season, and nothing on this earth lasts forever.

Change is a principle of creation. In short, everything changes.

The simple statement *everything changes* conveys a principle that can bring tremendous peace and understanding to us. If we accept the inevitable truth that nothing in our lives will remain the same, we can develop realistic levels of expectation and minimize our disappointments.

We generally experience four types of change in life: (1) change that happens around us, (2) change that happens to us, (3) change that happens within us, and (4) change that we make happen.

One of the greatest tragedies in life is that only a small percentage of the world's population responds to change effectively. Many people are victims of change. Some people dread change; others refuse to accept it. These approaches are formulas for frustration, depression, and wasted potential.

Are you teetering at the threshold of a new season? Change may make you feel more trepidation than trust. Yet you can learn to embrace change with a positive attitude and use it to benefit your life, as well as others' lives.

Or, perhaps you anticipate change in the future and are excited about it. As you read this book and come to view times of transition from a new perspective, you'll discover tremendous opportunities for personal, professional, and corporate growth. These new possibilities hold an exciting destiny for you.

Be bold and embrace the next season of your life. It's the only path to fulfilling your potential—and your unique contribution to your generation.

Lost opportunity means the sacrifice of destiny.

—Dr. Myles Munroe

INTRODUCTION
A Historic Convergence

The dogmas of the quiet past are inadequate to the stormy present.
—Abraham Lincoln

N o matter who you are—regardless of your country, race, ethnicity, language, and disposition—*time* and *change* will affect you.

Life is continually handing us personal, family, community, and national changes. However, we are also living in a time when there is a convergence of worldwide changes that is creating a transitional tide in human history. We are experiencing change on a big scale. In response, we must understand this change and meet it effectively or the forces of transition will pull us along, and we will have no influence in the midst of them.

Historic convergences and transitional tides have occurred at significant points throughout the ages. A historic convergence is a strategic period of history when major events occur, bringing with them momentous transformations in social, economic, political, and spiritual conditions. In the past, some strategic changes have been welcomed by people, while others have been dreaded. Certain changes have drawn mixed reactions from individuals. Unsettling times throughout history have resulted in societal fear, panic, distress, and confusion. Many people were not prepared for these changes; some reacted with suspicion, contempt, and violence, while others simply surrendered to the inevitable and became victims of the elements of change.

Let us look back through the corridor of time to various strategic points in history. Transitional periods occurred during the times known as the Dark Ages and the Enlightenment, during the times of the exploits of great explorers such as Christopher Columbus, during the western expansion of Europe to the Americas, colonization, the slave trade, the birth of the republic of the United States, World Wars I and II, the creation of the United Nations, the birth of the nation of Israel, the Civil Rights Movement, the decline of communism, the expansion of Islam, the birth and growth of new Eastern religions, and the emergence of international terrorism.

The nineteenth and twentieth centuries were noted for great changes in the arenas of science, technology, transportation, communication, education, and religion. The explosion of scientific discoveries led to advances in medicine and the invention of the telephone, airplane, radio, television, and computer. The development of intercontinental travel resulted in intercultural exposures not possible in earlier times. The world truly has become a "global village."

Change is in the air. It is everywhere.

This brief overview captures the complex nature of some of the events that have shaped the world in which we live today. As we move forward in the twenty-first century, we, also, are caught in transitional tides. Everyone with a measure of discernment, spiritual insight, and historical perspective can sense a historic convergence in every sphere of life. Change is in the air. It is everywhere. The present time period demands a response within the context of these changes. What is the nature of the transitions taking place at this juncture in history?

A quick assessment reveals tremendous change in the international political equation. We have seen the demise of colonialism, the extinction of the Cold War, the birth and rise of increasingly significant independent states (both large and small), an increase in worldwide economic interdependence, and global access to instant intercultural/international communication through the Internet. Post-World War II leaders have passed their leadership to younger generations who are removed from that era, bringing a youthfulness to national leadership not seen in some decades. In the Christian church, old guard Protestant and evangelical leaders and those who founded the charismatic movement are drifting from the scene. Their departure makes room for a new crop of leaders for the twenty-first century church.

Moreover, a significant shift is taking place in former colonial territories that were once the focus of mission efforts, many of which have been identified as undeveloped, developing, or Third World countries. The growth of the national church and church leadership within these nations requires a new approach for a new era.

In *The Principles and Benefits of Change: Fulfilling Your Purpose in Unsettled Times*, we will look at worldwide and personal challenges we all face today. We are truly in seasons of change. It will take an informed, globally minded, spiritually sensitive, skilled, educated, purpose-inspired person to effectively make a difference in our generation and set a standard for the generations to come. It will take those who understand the dynamics of change and who determine to respond rather than to react. Today's leaders will have to be creative on demand, understanding their roles and purposes in their generation.

The historic convergence discussed above is occurring in ten major areas. I believe the twenty-first century will be known as the age of:

1. Globalization
2. Information
3. Communication
4. Mobilization
5. Cultural Diversification
6. Mergers and Networking
7. Longevity of Life
8. Technology

9. Social and Political Transition
10. Rapid Transformation

A paradigm shift is taking place in these arenas, a trend that we will look at more closely in the chapter "Worldwide Tides of Change." Across the globe, leaders are sensing an urgency to integrate their nations into these changes. Old styles of leadership have lost their effectiveness and must yield to the new equation of twenty-first century leadership.

Moreover, the emergence of Third World leadership in the social, political, and religious fields is undeniable. The formerly opposed, rejected, and ignored are rising up to places of influence. This international change includes a shift in emphasis, priorities, and methods. Whether you live in a modern industrial society or in the developing Third World, you must carefully consider how these changes affect your life. It is imperative that we know how to prepare for the change, how to respond to the change, how to maximize the change, and what to do to change *ourselves* in order to fulfill our individual and corporate purposes.

> *On a global scale, as well as on a personal one, we must be prepared for transformation.*

On a global scale, therefore, as well as on a personal one, we must be prepared for transformation. Let us embrace the principles and benefits of change so we may fulfill our individual and corporate destinies, in all seasons and circumstances of our lives.

Neither a wise man nor a brave man lies down on the tracks of history to wait for the train of the future to run over him.
—Dwight D. Eisenhower

Part 1

THE CHANGE FACTOR

EVERYTHING CHANGES

An Inevitability Shared by Everyone on Earth

The future has a way of arriving unannounced.
—George Will, Pulitzer prize-winning journalist and author

While we live and breathe on this earth, 6.7 billion of us human beings share the same inevitability: we all have to face *change*. The same was true for everyone who existed in the past. The same will be true for everyone who will be born in the future.

Our lives are in a constant state of transition. Life is always moving forward; nothing ever remains the same. Even those who live essentially quiet lives are affected by change. To a greater or lesser degree, we are continually being transported—whether suddenly or gradually—into the new, the different, the unexpected, or the untried.

Change is one of the most important factors in life, whether that change is imposed on us or we've created the change ourselves and are eagerly anticipating its possibilities. Yet most people don't manage change effectively and positively. Some believe that change just "happens," and they don't think seriously about the effects change is having on them. Many also neglect to initiate positive changes that would make a significant difference in their lives and the lives of others. And the majority of us end up, in some way, the victims of unwanted change.

Four Types of Change

We experience four distinct types of change in life:

1. Change that happens *to us*—unexpected or anticipated change that affects our personal lives, families, careers, and so forth.

2. Change that happens *around us*—unexpected or anticipated change that affects our society, nation, or world and that also has some impact on us personally or on our ways of life.

3. Change that happens *within us*—unexpected or anticipated change that directly affects who we are—either physically, emotionally, mentally, or spiritually.

4. Change that *we initiate*—something created or altered by plans we have implemented in order to move us from the present to a preferred future.

We can identify each of the above as a distinct type of change, even though, sometimes, there may be overlap between them.

What Are the Results of Change?

Change transports the present into a future that demands a response.

Change transports the present into a future that demands a response. Often, that response requires further change from us. The fact of the needed change may bring positive activity—excitement, anticipation, and energetic planning. Or, it may bring a negative reaction—uncertainty, stress, and emotional shutdown. How we react to change has greater consequences to us than we may realize.

Imagine that you were transported a hundred years into the future. The changes that would have taken place in your nation and the world would be such that you would hardly recognize your own community. Abruptly coming into a transformed world would be a drastic encounter with change. Almost everything you are familiar with on a day-to-day basis would be gone: family, friends, culture, ways of interacting with the world (such as technology, communication), ways of perceiving the world (socially, politically, economically), and so forth. The language would even have evolved. Your words and even speech patterns would seem quaint to those in the twenty-second century. You would be as disoriented as someone from the first decade of the twentieth century trying to figure out what an iPod is.

In the movie *The Shawshank Redemption*, one of the characters, Brooks, is paroled from the penitentiary. Brooks hasn't lived out in society for five decades. He went to prison during the first decade of the twentieth century and is released in the 1950s. He considers harming or even killing a fellow inmate because then he will be charged with assault or murder and be able to stay in prison. His friends talk him out of it, however, and he is released from the penitentiary as scheduled. Brooks boards the bus that will take him into town, where he will live at a halfway house and work at a grocery store, bagging groceries. The bus speeds up to probably thirty-five or forty miles per hour, but Brooks clutches tightly to the seat railing because the speed is overwhelming to him. His expression of fear contrasts with the rest of the passengers on the bus, who just look bored. Brooks has no frame of reference for what the others take completely for granted. "I can't believe how fast things move on the outside," he writes to his friends. Everything about his life is unfamiliar, foreign. Brooks has nightmares in which he is falling. "I'm tired of being afraid all the time," he says.

Change and Loss

Gradual change, experienced on a daily basis, is relatively easy for people to handle. Often, they don't even notice it. But sudden change can affect people in a way similar to Brooks' experience. Depending on the intensity of the change—and the resulting loss—the effects of change can vary from merely stretching someone to grow a little to causing someone to experience such mental conflict between past and present that he or she succumbs to a breakdown or even commits suicide. That's what happens to Brooks in *Shawshank Redemption*. He can't handle living on "the outside," and, tragically, he takes his own life. Commenting on Brooks' situation, another character, Red, gestures to the prison walls surrounding the outside courtyard and says, "I'm telling you, these walls are funny. At first, you hate 'em. Then, you get used to 'em. Enough time passes, you get so you depend on 'em."

Similarly, the effects of failing to implement positive change to improve one's life can range from someone missing out on a single rewarding experience to not fulfilling his or her entire purpose for living.

In most of the above scenarios, the person reacting negatively to change experiences loss. Mostly, it is the loss of potential. It's the loss of what that person could have been or done by responding constructively to change. This is why it is essential for us to learn to oversee change rather than become its victims, and why we must initiate change rather than be left behind by it.

The ongoing dynamic of change is one of the most important factors of human life.

The ongoing dynamic of change, therefore, is one of the most important factors of human life. How we relate to change has a significant impact on our quality of life and whether or not we accomplish what we are meant to during our time on earth. Understanding how to view, respond to, and benefit from change is vital to a well-balanced and fulfilled life.

Five Principles of Change

Let's consider five foundational principles of *change* and their implications:

1. **Nothing on earth is as permanent as change.** What a paradox! One thing that's always present on this earth is change. Nothing else can really be expected or guaranteed.

2. **Change is continual.** Our lives keep moving forward, and the environment around us undergoes alterations all the time. Change doesn't stop when we sleep, when we take a vacation, or when we're on a lunch break. Change is ceaseless.

3. **Everything changes.** The details of our lives are always in transition. Here are just some of the ways in which your life will (or can) change:

+ Your *knowledge* will change. We are always taking in more knowledge and information from a variety of sources. Often, the more information we receive, the more we view life and other people differently. New knowledge will change your perspectives or broaden or deepen your original ideas.

+ Your *interests* will change. Some of the things you are interested in today may change tomorrow as you expand the range of your experiences. Or, you may decide to focus on just one or two areas of interest in order to achieve a particular goal, putting other interests on the back burner or dropping them altogether.

+ Your *values and priorities* will change. The things that you value now may not be the things that you will value in the next ten years, five years, or one year. I don't necessarily mean core life values, although these may change. Rather, I'm referring more to the priority or value we place on certain people or things. This may change due to increased personal maturity or to the particular stage of life we are in. For example, when many couples get married and start families, they begin to think about pursuing spiritual values because they think it will be good for their children. Or, the change may have to do with temporary life circumstances. Perhaps you had been focusing on building a vacation house, but you lost your job and are now focused just on keeping your primary home. Your plans have had to be cancelled or postponed. You don't value that vacation house as a priority anymore because something more important has taken its place. When your values change, it can change your whole lifestyle.

+ Your *body* will change. If you are a young person, you are still growing and maturing into an adult. If you are already an adult, you will notice various physical changes as you grow older: your hairline recedes; your eyes don't focus as they used to, and you have to buy reading glasses; your strength and flexibility are not what they had been; and so forth. These types of changes can significantly impact the quality of our lives if we are unprepared for them.

+ Your *family relationships network* will change. We don't really know how our relationships may change in any given year. You may gain a new family member through a marriage or a birth. Sometimes, life hits you broadside; you didn't even know it was coming, but suddenly, you've lost a family member through divorce or death. Perhaps a parent or grandparent develops Alzheimer's or has to move into a nursing home. These are among the most difficult changes we can experience.

+ Your *marriage* will change. The dynamics of your marriage relationship will change over time. This doesn't mean that your marriage is wrong or bad, but only that people and situations undergo transformation. Over the years, you will change and grow, and so will your spouse. We have to expect, prepare for, and get used to those changes. Changes in marital relationships can happen anytime. Yet much has been written about what happens to couples when their children go to college or move into their own homes. How do a husband and a wife learn to relate to each another again as two people—without the constant presence of children in the home? Or perhaps the husband has been the breadwinner of the family for twenty years and is suddenly laid off. How will this change in income and standard of living, even if temporary, affect the marriage? Can the couple keep a strong relationship if there needs to be a work adjustment for months or even years? Some people also experience unwanted divorce. These and many other factors affect the marriage relationship.

+ Your *children* will change. The image of their children as infants is indelible in most parents' minds. When you bring your children home from the hospital after they are born, you must care for their every need. Yet they will move toward independence as they grow older. When your daughter turns eleven, for example, she may not want to wear that shirt you bought her but would rather make her own clothing choices. At sixteen, your son may want to stay out with his friends as long as he likes. Teenagers still need structure and loving guidance, but you have to learn how to adjust to their equally important need to grow up. Sometimes, we still want to treat them as if they are three years old. When your children mature and desire independence, you have to learn to handle this change with skill.

+ Your *friends* will change. While certain friendships can last a life-time, the people with whom we spend a lot of time at one point in our lives may not be close to us later on, either geographically or emotionally. This may be due to a move, a divorce, or a shift in priorities. This adjustment may be difficult for you, especially if the friend is one with whom you grew up or one to whom you had been extremely close. Then, you may "outgrow" certain people because you are going in a new direction in life, with goals or in-terests that these friends don't share or value. At times, you have to relinquish some mere acquaintances so that you can gain new friends. Finally, some friendships may undergo change because the friends are just not healthy for you—your "friends" are encourag-ing you to do something self-destructive or illegal. We must expect that our friendships will change once in a while.

+ Your *job* may change. You can't always control where you work, or whether you will be at your job for any specific length of time. Do you have the mental, emotional, and financial resources to handle a change in job status?

4. *Change is inevitable*. No one on earth can avoid change. This conclu-sion is not easy for some people to accept. Nevertheless, we must come to acknowledge that change *is* inevitable. When I settled this fact in my own heart and mind, my life became much easier to live. It is not healthy for us to believe that life will always remain the same. Everything may be going on an even plane right now, but there will be a transition or a point of stress in the future. Life is full of the unexpected, and changes will come upon us, at some time or another.

5. *Change is a principle of life and creation*. This last statement is really a summation of all the above: change is a principle of life. It is the way the world functions. It affects everybody. In one sense, change is proof that you are alive! Everything that you go through is a manifestation of some type of change, and it's just a part of life.

The Human Equalizer

These principles of change highlight the fact that change is a human "equalizer." Nobody has a monopoly on change. Change affects everybody on the planet, no matter who they are. I know a man who is worth hundreds of millions of dollars but found out he had a serious illness that none of his doctors could cure. When he told me this, I thought, *Change really affects us all.* Sometimes, people think that if they had riches, it would keep them immune from change, but that isn't true.

I imagine there's another man in a hospital right now who is facing the same illness but doesn't have money to pay his household bills, let alone his hospital fees. Yet the same change in health in both these men's lives—one a millionaire, the other broke—puts them on an equal plane. Change does that.

So, change is every human being's experience. If you think things aren't changing in your life right now, just wait a week or a month or a year. Wealth, youth, talent, intelligence, popularity, success, ambition, or good intentions don't make you immune: no matter who you are, you will experience it. So, whenever you encounter change—especially change you consider disruptive or distressing—don't feel you're all alone in this. We are all subject to change!

We're Double-Minded toward Change

Since change is inevitable and all pervasive in our lives, why is it that so many people react to it as if it is a threat? When we see change all around us, why do we expect things to remain the same (except, perhaps, when we're the ones attempting the change)? There are significant reasons for this, which we will explore in coming chapters. But let's consider one facet of the question now: our double-mindedness toward change.

In many ways, people live contentedly with change and welcome it: they want to wear the latest styles, use the newest technological innovations, employ easier methods for accomplishing everyday tasks, and so on. During presidential elections in the United States, people are often asked by political candidates, "Are you better off than you were four years ago?" If they don't feel they are, they will likely vote for the candidate they believe can bring positive change to the country.

Some people like nostalgia. They may wear "retro" clothing, watch vintage television programs, or buy furniture reminiscent of an earlier time period. Yet most of them would not really want to live in those times. They enjoy the latest technology. They like convenience. They welcome innovation—even if these new things make older things obsolete or if the innovations were developed under the pressures of economic necessity. Yet when change comes into their lives in a way they didn't expect or want, they take it personally—even though, sometimes, some of the same societal forces may be at work creating the inconvenience as much as the convenience. We like change as long as it doesn't cause *us* any discomfort.

We are therefore double-minded about change. "Good" change can come, but we should never have to deal with what we perceive as unpleasant or negative change.

We're Not Taught to Deal with Change

One of the reasons for our double-mindedness is that no one ever sat us down and said, "You know, things never stay the same. Change is going to happen, and you have to learn to respond to it and use it for your benefit." Parents don't teach this idea to their children. Schools don't include it in their curriculum. People aren't naturally skilled in it. It's not an instinct within us. We learn about change the hard way—by experience. Yet most of us never learn to respond to it effectively.

In a similar way, many people have never been taught that they need to develop certain skills to be able to *initiate* changes that will improve their lives. Even if people desire positive change, they are hindered from obtaining it by fear and uncertainty, or because they act rashly instead of purposefully and wisely.

Is Change Working for You?

What is your experience with change in your life? Do you generally feel that change is working for you—or do you feel that its influences are working against you? Do you know how to turn negative change to your benefit? To what extent have you been initiating positive change in your life?

The following are five ways in which people typically approach change.

Five Approaches to Change

1. *People watch things happen.* This is a passive, indifferent approach in which people don't react to change because they have no real interest in it or its impact.

2. *People let things happen.* This is a resigned, defeated, or even fatalistic approach. A person may lash out against the change, but ultimately, his or her mind-set is, "There's nothing I can do about this."

3. *People ask, "What happened?"* This is an inquisitive response, but it doesn't go much further than mere curiosity or an interest in the latest gossip. It can also mean that a person never saw the change coming, and therefore he or she wasn't prepared to respond to it.

4. *People defy what happens.* This is when someone tries to resist inevitable change in his or her life, wasting valuable time and energy in the process.

5. *People make things happen.* This is a proactive response by people that either alters the quality or degree of change that happens to the person or that initiates new change. Proactive people are the ones who usually succeed in life—against all odds. I refer to these men and women as "world changers."

You will never really know who you are—and who you can be—if you don't understand the nature of change and understand how to shape its consequences. With each change that happens to us, around us, or within us, we can...

1. Learn to define and interpret the change.

2. Discover principles for responding to the change so that it benefits ourselves or others.

With each change we wish to initiate in our lives, we can...

1. Learn how creating change enables us to fulfill our purposes in life.

2. Discover practical methods for implementing specific plans to fulfill those purposes.

Change—Enemy or Friend?

Think of change as your friend rather than your enemy. Change is not the kind of "friend" who will sit and commiserate with you at a pity party but a friend who will encourage you to be the best you can be. It is my desire that, through this book, you will begin to see change as the arrival of opportunity rather than an invasion of destruction.

Responding to change in a positive way doesn't come automatically or easily for most people. Yet there are specific principles of change that enable us to deal with and benefit from it. The only way for you to move forward to where you want to go in life, regardless of your circumstances, is to initiate desired change and to address unwanted change constructively. You must understand the nature of change and the principles for responding to it. Otherwise, you will be sidetracked or defeated by times of transition and perhaps never make the personal and professional advances needed to improve your life.

> *The only way for you to move forward is to initiate desired change and to address unwanted change constructively.*

Yes, *everything changes*. Now, let's explore how to make change work for you.

You cannot step twice into the same river, for other waters are continually flowing in.
—Heraclitus, Greek philosopher

REACTING TO CHANGE
Our Natural Tendency: Acting before Thinking

If you don't like change, you're going to like irrelevance even less.
—General Eric Shinseki, former U.S. Army Chief of Staff

To live fulfilling and productive lives, we must discover how to oversee change—both that which comes to us and that which we initiate. We must know how to plan for and use change for our benefit.

Reacting to Change versus Responding to Change

Since most people don't prepare for change, however, the average person doesn't *respond* to change—he *reacts* to it. In this sense, I'm defining *reaction* as having a negative attitude toward change, or taking an action against change before really thinking about it or its consequences. This is the most detrimental way to handle change. It usually results in fear, miscalculation, overcompensation, premature activity, irresponsible or unnecessary use of resources, and even disaster. Merely *reacting* to change essentially gives change the advantage over you, rendering you a victim of your circumstances.

You can be learn to be stronger than what happens to you when unexpected change occurs. The first way to do this is to understand the difference between *reacting* to change and *responding* to change. There is a vast difference between the two.

Ways People React to Change

In chapter 1, we looked at five ways people approach change: they (1) watch change happen, (2) let change happen, (3) ask, "What happened?" (4) defy what happens, and (5) make change happen. Note that the first four are all *reactions* to change. When change happens to you, around you, or within you, you have to be wise in how you deal with it. Again, many people experience immediate confusion, fear, desperation, or anger when they confront change—and, as a result, they act in negative ways that reflect these feelings. If we are to benefit from change, we must understand our role in the process and work with it rather than against it.

What do you do if you're pulled by tides of change that you really have no control over?

Let's take a closer look at various *reactions* people can have to unexpected or unwanted change, which we must guard against as unproductive and destructive. Then, we'll look at five positive *responses* to change that will enable us to turn any situation into something beneficial.

You Can Ignore or Deny Change

When change threatens our comfort and security, we're tempted to retreat into a world of denial.

Ignoring or denying change is the worst reaction you can have toward change. When change threatens our comfort and security, we're tempted to retreat into a world of denial. In an attempt to protect our fragile sense of comfort, security, or importance, we create a world of our own making rather than accept what is happening in the real world. In fact, ignoring change is actually an acknowledgment of it because you don't ignore something that isn't there! Moreover, pretending that change isn't happening has no effect on change. It usually just makes you a victim of it.

No matter the source of change—be it personal, social, political, economic, or spiritual—we can't pretend that the change is not happening. When it occurs, do not deny it. Instead, seek to understand it, accept its reality, and commit to fulfilling the new role it demands from you. Sometimes, to deny change means to minimize the value of what's emerging. It also means that you don't give change the place it deserves in the overall scheme of things. In a sense, to deny change means to disrespect reality, to make no room to accommodate it. It means that you insist on continuing business as usual, when it's no longer usual. You live in an imaginary world that has no relevance to the world that has come into being because you have determined that the past is better than the future. Change is always the introduction of the future to the present. Change is tomorrow taking over today, and a denial of change is a decision to live in yesterday.

Eventually, to deny change is to become irrelevant.

The largest island in the Bahamas is Andros, and it's famous for its abundance of crabs. Bahamians love to eat crabs; they're considered a wonderful delicacy. The Bahamas have both sea crabs and land crabs, and most of the people who live on Andros are well known for harvesting land crabs, which they sell locally.

People normally go crabbing at night because the crabs hide in their holes during the day but come out at night in order to feed. My first experience with crabbing was when I was young, and my friends and I went crabbing on Andros, which was a fun group thing to do. We were going through the rocks and the bushes at night, and people were catching crabs. At one point, one of my close friends and I came into an area where we saw a number of crabs. To catch crabs in the bush, you use a flashlight. When you shine the light on the crabs, they freeze because they're shocked by the sudden bright light. For a few minutes, they won't move, as if they are paralyzed. After we shined the light on the crabs and they froze, they did something I'd never seen before. They closed their eyes. I asked my friend, "Why do they shut their eyes when you shine the light on them?" He said, "Because the crabs believe that if *they* can't see you, *you* can't see them. And so we catch them."

These crabs remind me of people who attempt to ignore change. Change comes upon them, sometimes in a startling or blinding way. Yet, instead of reorienting themselves to its glare, they imagine that if they close their eyes to it, then the change can't "see" them and therefore won't affect them. But the sad result is that change will then "catch" them and take them away with it, making them mere statistics of change. Denial is the worst reaction you can ever have to change because you *do nothing*.

You Can Become Angry at Change

Becoming angry is also a dangerous reaction to change. Nothing is as immobilizing as an angry spirit. It produces irrational behavior and self-destructive decisions. The familiarity of the past can make the prospect of a new future unsettling, causing a person to attack rather than to embrace the potential of promise.

Many people become angry because change comes without their permission, and it's not something they want or feel able to deal with. Yet being angry at inevitable change is like being angry at winter for coming. If you live in a climate with winters characterized by snow, sleet, and ice, then these things are sure to come every year. If you are angry at winter, you just lose time and energy, for your anger achieves nothing.

Among other negative outcomes, being angry at change can lead you to...

+ Develop internal stress. This can cause you to become physically sick.

+ Become bitter. This will eat at you emotionally, physically, and spiritually.

+ Turn on the very people you love. You may begin to verbally attack your family members and friends.

+ Accuse people who are not responsible for it. You may blame others and may even become antagonistic against society in general. In this way, instead of becoming a part of the solution, you become another problem.

+ Develop self-destructive habits. You don't want to deal with the change, so you begin to take up unhealthy practices, such as drinking to excess or taking drugs.

Even though you perceive a change as negative—and it may, indeed, have cost you something valuable—becoming angry will only hurt you further. It will not make anything better.

What can we do about it? We can be honest with ourselves and life. We can understand the value of both our past and present roles. Each of us is important to the Creator's great program of purpose in this world, and His purposes continue in our lives, even though circumstances and people change.

You Can Defy or Resist Change

When I refer to defying or resisting change as a negative reaction, I'm not talking about responding to problems that can be addressed, such as cleaning up corruption and bringing justice to those who are being taken advantage of. I'm referring specifically to change that you cannot, for all practical purposes, do anything about. For example, maybe your company goes completely out of business and you lose your job, or perhaps your spouse divorces you and marries someone else. You can't "resist" this kind of change in the way you might resist the spread of crime in your neighborhood. When this type of uncontrollable, irreversible change happens to you, you have a choice about how to react. Some people get into "fight mode." This goes beyond their being angry and turning on themselves and others. It means that they decide they will defy the reality of circumstances, situations, and events that are impacting their present states.

People lose out on opportunities to explore the uncharted territories of their true potential—all for the sake of trying to protect the way life used to be.

You can actually say to yourself about such change, *This **will not** happen.* You can resolve in your heart that you will die holding on to your previous status or situation, whether or not it truly exists any longer. Some people who have gone through the heartbreak of divorce still try to win back their former spouses when the ex-spouses have already remarried and gone on to new lives without looking back. Other people have lost their jobs when the industries they've been working in have become obsolete, yet they still hold on to the idea that they may someday get their old jobs back. The tragic thing is that they end up sacrificing the rest of their lives to their lost pasts. They lose out on opportunities to enjoy the relationships they still have, to meet new friends, to expand their knowledge, and to explore the uncharted territories of their true potential—all for the sake of trying to protect the way life used to be.

You can try to resist certain inevitable forces of change, but change will always win.

You Can "Accept" Change

To accept change means that you acknowledge change is coming or is already happening. You assess the impact of that change on your life, your environment, and your circumstances. Even though this acknowledgment is good, it is still only the first step to responding effectively to change. For example, imagine that a train is coming on a track on which you are standing, and you say to yourself, *That train is moving toward me, and I accept the fact that it is traveling at a high speed, and I accept the fact that I cannot stop it, and that it will hit me.* If you merely accept the train's approach without moving out of its way, you are at the mercy of that locomotive. This is why acceptance alone can still be detrimental. Many people who accept change become victims of that change. So, if you stop at the acceptance of change, you will not reap any real benefit; your acceptance will end up as another form of reaction rather than as a true response to change. It won't transform your life in any positive way.

You Can Adjust to or Accommodate Change

Adjusting to or accommodating inevitable change means you are aware that if you don't do something, the change will have a permanent impact on you, and it may be one that is detrimental to you. Therefore, you alter a few things in your life to adapt to it. Yet this approach doesn't result in your really benefiting from the change because you simply accommodated it. In other words, you did not actively use that change for your advantage. Adjusting to change will not allow you to be transformed by it or to turn the change to your benefit. That's not enough. Even if you accept and adjust to change, you can still end up being its victim because you are not at the point of truly interacting with it.

You Can Become a Victim of Change

Any of the above approaches to change can result in someone allowing himself or herself to become a "victim" of change. Again, being a victim of change means that your reaction to it leaves you as a mere statistic. If you don't interact with change, you become a by-product of its effects.

If you are thirty-five or younger, life without computers may be hard to imagine. Yet, sometime in the future, an innovation will come along that your generation isn't fully prepared for. It happens to every generation, affecting even those who believe they will *always* be on the cutting edge of technology and culture. And computers are still a stumbling block for some older baby boomers. Suppose you had worked in a factory for twenty-five years, starting in 1965. When you began working there, they had no computers. You counted products in the warehouse by hand and you wrote them down on a piece of paper. Then, you started using a calculator, but you still had to put the numbers in a ledger. In the meantime, you gained a degree of seniority in the company. Yet, now, when you're twenty-five years into the job, the head office says, "We are going to computerize the warehouse, and everybody must learn to use a computer."

Here you are, forty-eight years old, you've never used a computer before, you don't even understand them, but you want to keep your job. You love this company, and you appreciate the way they've been good to you and your family over the years. What do you do? You could react in any of the ways we've just discussed.

You could try to ignore it, thinking, *I'm not interested in learning the computer; I'm too old to learn; I don't want to go back to school to prepare for another field. I'll just go along doing my job as I always have.* Of course, the company would bring you back to reality by telling you that you either had to learn the computer or stop receiving a paycheck.

You could become angry about the situation and stomp around the warehouse, yelling at the management, then lash out at your spouse when you go home. But that wouldn't enable you to keep your job, either.

You could resist it, saying, "I refuse to learn the computer. I don't care what they say." Of course, again, you would be let go.

You could accept the fact that the company needs to improve, saying, "We need to have a better way of keeping track of the numbers, but although I accept the fact that we need the computer upgrade, I'm still not willing to learn it." Same result.

Any of these reactions will lead to your being a victim of the change. The company will say, "If you are not able to tap into the computer system for inventory control and analysis, then you are redundant."

The changing nature of business, industry, trade, and economics around the world, with the accompanying loss of jobs and creation of new ones, is causing people to have to confront new employment situations and realities. Those who were trained in certain fields or jobs that are no longer viable are not skilled or educated in new areas that could open up employment for them. Many are afraid to learn new skills.

> *Millions of people are allowing themselves to fall into a state of victimization when they have the ability to respond rather than react to change.*

Yet change is not just about jobs and economics. Through *all* types of change—and in a myriad of ways—millions of people are allowing themselves to fall into a state of victimization when they have the ability to respond rather than react to change.

Victims of change, therefore, have been swallowed up by a tsunami of transition. The undercurrent pulls their lives out to sea and then batters them against the rocks of reality. Then, their hopes, aspirations, and dreams are left gasping for breath on the shores of humanity.

To use another analogy, when we do not anticipate change or understand how to respond to it, we become like pawns in a chess game in which "Change" is playing against "The Way It Used to Be." And "Change" is always winning.

What Will You Do with Change?

Since life involves a continual series of transitions, we should endeavor to be always prepared to respond to change.

If you react, you are a victim. If you respond, you are a victor.

If you react, change leads your life. If you respond, *you* lead change in your life.

The only defense against the negative impact of change is the anticipation of, and preparation for, its inevitability. The ability to respond rather than react puts you in control and reduces change to servanthood. Responding to change gives you the ability to use change for your benefit.

Resolve to be a master of change rather than a victim of change.
—Brian Tracy, best-selling author, speaker, and business consultant

RESPONDING TO CHANGE
Essential Life Skills: Preparing for the Unexpected, Initiating Purpose

Change is inevitable, except from vending machines.
—Anonymous

Nothing is more secure than the familiar. Being creatures of habit, many people dread the thought of change. Yet since change is a principle of life, we must learn to live with it—more than that, we must discover how to benefit from it. Responding rather than reacting to change enables you to grow stronger for the next phase of your life.

We have seen that even if you refuse to change, change will affect you. Change will happen *to* you, *with* you, *around* you, and *without* you. When the leaves change color and fall off the trees in autumn, and the weather gets colder, everyone knows what season is coming. Being prepared for winter protects you against its potentially harmful effects while enabling you to benefit from it. You buy a warm coat before the first frost so you can wear it on chilly days. You stock up on salt or sand so you can pour it on your outside steps, walkway, and driveway to prevent yourself from slipping when it gets icy. You may also obtain a pair of skis or ice skates so you can benefit from winter's snow and ice as means of entertainment and exercise. In order to have something constructive to do when the weather gets too cold to work outside, you might plan a special project of finally putting those old photos into albums or perhaps stockpile seed catalogs so you can look through them in preparation for spring planting. When you are prepared, you can approach winter with a feeling of confidence rather than apprehension.

Knowing how to respond to inevitable change can keep you at peace during any change you may experience.

Knowing how to respond to inevitable change rather than just reacting to it can keep you at peace during any change you may experience. If you are to engage fully in life, then you must not ignore the truth about the future. It holds one of two options for you: respond effectively to change or be a victim of change.

You have the power to determine the quality and effectiveness of your future by your response to change.

In the last chapter, we saw that while accepting change is the first step toward responding, if we go no further than acceptance, we will still end up as victims. Let's look now at ways in which we can respond rather than react to change.

Ways to Respond to Change

You Can Oversee Change

Overseeing, or managing, change means that you have recognized and acknowledged change but are also taking some practical steps to address it. You are currently engaged in assessing how you can best control its impending impact on your life. You don't necessarily avoid the problem, but you try to direct its effects on your life, your environment, and your circumstances, thereby minimizing any negative results. You're still not yet positioning yourself to benefit or use it effectively. You're simply controlling it. Overseeing change is better than reacting in the ways we discussed in the previous chapter, but it's still not enough.

You Can Integrate Yourself in Change

Integrating yourself in change means that when change is happening to you, you become an active participator in its unfolding. This doesn't necessarily mean that you approve of it or support it. However, you understand that it is a reality and position yourself to move forward in life in the midst of it. If you do support it, then you actively seek to help the change to take place. You embrace it and search for your place in it.

Some overwhelming tides of change will flow through your life or your society, and you must adapt to them and participate in the transition process instead of fighting them. After the resurrection of Jesus of Nazareth, His disciples preached His message boldly, and an angry crowd wanted to put them to death. Yet Gamaliel, who was a Pharisee and a teacher of the law, warned the religious community, *"If it is from God, you will not be able to stop these men; you will only find yourselves fighting against God"* (Acts 5:39).

Likewise, we can't fight change when the hand of the God is truly in it. In such cases, we must demonstrate the maturity required for responding effectively in times of transition. In part 3, we will focus on how we can fulfill the purposes the Creator has for our lives and how change relates to those purposes. For now, let's remind ourselves of what first century theologian Paul of Tarsus wrote: *"We know that in all things God works for the good of those who love him, who have been called according to his purpose"* (Romans 8:28). We can become a part of God's process, which always works for our good when we are aligned with His purposes. When we are in step with His plans, we can have confidence in any situation, however unsettling.

You must, therefore, be proactive when such changes are taking place. You don't want to *let* change happen—you want to *help* change happen. Those who will survive and benefit in the midst of change are those who understand their places in the process and participate fully in what the change was intended to deliver. The danger, again, is the temptation to ignore change and be idle.

For example, when political change is ushered in by an election and one party is replaced by another, there are usually some people in the "losing" party who separate themselves from the transition instead of remaining involved in the process. They say, for example, "I'm not getting involved," or

"I'm not voting anymore," or "I'm not going to work with these people." The only problem is that change will happen either with you or without you. It is the process of life. So, those who decide to bide their time in the midst of change are like a man standing in the middle of a blizzard and wearing his swim trunks, hoping that the temperature will rise to 85 degrees. Of course, there will be a funeral. Instead of integrating himself into the new season by wearing winter clothes or seeking refuge indoors, he allows the change of weather to kill him.

We talked above about the futility of fighting against the hand of God. Similarly, we can be tempted to just withdraw from active participation in God's purposes as a way of expressing our dissatisfaction with His will. This dangerous attitude says, "If I am not in charge and in control, then I will not get involved." This is an immature, fatalistic mentality that reduces one to becoming part of the problem rather than a part of the provision in God's plan. This is why it is essential that we all find our places in God's program and fulfill our life purposes, no matter what new roles they may involve.

You Can Prepare and Plan for Change

Those who prepare and plan for change are never really surprised by it because they understand that change is integral to life.

This is one of the highest levels of response to change. Those who prepare and plan for change are never really surprised by it because they understand that change is integral to life. If you understand the nature of change, you always expect it. Therefore, the best "response" to changes that happen to you, around you, and within you is to anticipate them ahead of time, because you can prepare only for what you expect. Change can often be sudden and surprising, and you don't always know specifically what to plan for. Yet a constructive response to the inevitability of change is to prepare your mind, your emotions, your family, your finances, and so forth for a number of eventualities.

If you don't learn to expect change, you will inevitably react to it when it occurs. You won't be able to respond to it effectively. A clear understanding that life will change is the key to preparing and planning for times of transition. It is this response of preparation that will give you control over change.

Planning enables you to go beyond mere oversight of change when it arrives. Instead, you can orchestrate it to work for your benefit. You can put in place sound overall plans, motivated by the mind-set that change is a way of life. This is the essence of *response to change*, as opposed to *reaction to change*, because it requires forethought.

To sum up, by planning and preparing for change, you...

+ reduce anxiety, stress, and fear.

+ gain greater control over your circumstances and environment.

+ increase your confidence.

+ make change your servant.

Planning and preparation are the evidence of foresight. They help produce internal peace for those who practice them, while others cower in chaos.

I have learned to avoid becoming unsettled, anxious, or angry about change by expecting it and always having a contingency plan. If there is nothing I can do about a certain situation, I put a plan into action to turn it to my advantage. This method can be used for both small inconveniences and critical events. Let's take a small change as illustration. Suppose I'm waiting to board a plane to go speak at a conference in Peru. As I sit at the gate, I hear an announcement that my plane has been delayed for two hours. Immediately, I open up my laptop and start reviewing my notes for my talk or planning material for a new talk. I never think twice about the situation as a "problem." While everyone else is sitting around complaining, I'm producing something.

You have to prepare yourself not only for what you want to happen, but also for what could happen.

I plan for this type of eventuality all the time, and I try always to think in terms of restructuring my situation to help me further my goals. I've trained myself, as I go through my day, to continually think ahead to what kind of change might happen to me and how I can best respond. This is not worrying; it's constructive preparation. There is a vital difference between the two. You have to prepare yourself not only for what you *want* to happen, but also for what *could* happen. That way, change never catches you off guard and you're not confused or immobilized, at least for long.

I've watched people "lose it" because they didn't expect that a particular situation could ever happen—especially to them. That's the power of the unexpected. It can dislodge you from your sense of security and rob you of your peace. It can destroy what you claim to have faith in because you didn't anticipate a challenge to your belief.

Again, you must expect change and plan and prepare for its eventuality because what you expect can never really surprise or disappoint you.

You Can Initiate Change

Initiating change is the highest level of response to change. We will discuss this point in more detail in later chapters, so that you can learn to apply it in practical ways—including how to discover your God-given purpose. When you initiate change, you are responding to change by realizing its potential and power and by actively creating it to further your vision and goals for your life based on your purpose.

To initiate change means the following: (1) You determine what changes in your life and environment will best serve the purposes you have been called to fulfill on this earth. (2) You order your life and environment according to these best interests. In other words, your unique assignment from the Creator produces the incentive to create the conditions and to gather the resources that will produce the changes necessary to fulfill His will for your life.

Be a World Changer

I challenge you to become someone who initiates change, who makes things happen to fulfill your purpose and who contributes your particular gifts to your generation. There are people who say, "I'm open to change as long as it doesn't affect me, as long as it doesn't cost me anything." But all change will cost something, even if it's just the loss of the familiar. We must be willing to let go of what *isn't* working for us in order to pursue what is best for us.

Are you willing to let go of the past and become proactive about the future? If so, you are ready to become a world changer.

> *I am always doing that which I can not do, in order that I may learn how to do it.*
> —Pablo Picasso, painter and sculptor

PROTECTION AGAINST CHANGE
Safeguards against Disappointment and Frustration

*Time changes everything except something within us which is
always surprised by change.*
—Thomas Hardy, novelist and poet

I n order to plan for change effectively, you must anticipate it continually. This sounds simple enough, but most of us don't do it. Because we naturally expect life to remain the same, we are caught off guard when things change. I've seen this oversight undermine the lives of many people. The principle of *anticipating* change is so crucial to understanding and dealing with change that we must constantly remind ourselves of it in order to internalize it. In this chapter, we will explore further how to counteract the negative effects of the unanticipated.

The "Timely" Lesson of the Swiss Watch Company

For more than a century, the undisputed world leader in the timepiece industry was the Swiss Watch Company. In fact, the word *watch* became synonymous with Switzerland. Their success as the most efficient watchmakers in the world went unchallenged. Everyone wanted a Swiss watch.

At the height of its reign as the king of the timepiece world, the Swiss Watch Company controlled more than 80 percent of the market. During this time, one of its young researchers, along with a number of his colleagues, invented a new, more accurate, and entirely electronic watch. The excited, youthful inventor was invited to introduce his latest brainchild at a specially called company board meeting. He hoped to secure the Swiss Watch Company's place as the leader in the watch sales market in the future.

As the inventor introduced the new product, the members of the board listened with interest and carefully assessed the idea of changing from a motorized- to an electronic-based product. After close review, the members decided the invention was interesting and held promise, but they refused to make it a priority. Why? They were satisfied with their century-long success in the world market. Unfortunately, their overly comfortable position contributed to their failure to patent the electronic watch.

A year later, the Swiss Watch Company displayed the new invention, along with its other products, at the Annual Watch Congress, and representatives of two companies noticed it. These two companies soon developed a similar prototype based on the principle of electronic operations, and marketed it. It revolutionized the watch industry worldwide.

The Swiss Watch Company never fully recovered from this shift in watch design. Today, the competition is shared among a number of companies that struggle to stay in the game. Ten years after the introduction of electronic watches to the marketplace, the Swiss Watch Company had less than 10 percent of world sales. This devastating loss forced the company to terminate fifty thousand of its sixty-five thousand employees. It plummeted from the pinnacle to the pits in just ten years.

The invention of the electric watch signaled a new season, a glimpse into the future, but a century of success had blinded the Swiss Watch Company's executives to the impending, inevitable reality of change.

The company board thought its manufacturing method was the only or best way to make a watch. It assumed that past success guaranteed future profits. Therefore, it ignored the prospect of competition from the effects of continual change. Their old methods kept them from embracing and benefiting from new ones.

The story of the Swiss Watch Company is a lesson for all of us: *ignoring a season of change can cause us to forfeit our God-given purposes. He who fails to expect, plan for, embrace, and oversee change will regret his past in the future.*

Our safeguard against the detrimental effects of unprepared-for events and circumstances is to continually *expect* change to occur in all areas of life. Grasping just this one truth will prepare you to handle many of the challenges that accompany change.

> *Our safeguard against unprepared-for events and circumstances is to continually expect change to occur in all areas of life.*

The Present Has a "Shelf Life"

In light of the above, we must come to accept the often sobering reality that whatever we are enjoying and using right now is only temporary. The expiration dates on food, medications, and other products tell us that after a certain time, the items will become spoiled or ineffective. After a while, their limited time frames of usefulness will be past. While they may last beyond the specified date, eventually, they will become useless.

Just as every product has a shelf life, the present has a "shelf life." Again, the way you currently think and what you're currently doing will change over time, at least to some degree. If it doesn't, you're not growing and maturing as a person! We all learn new things and come into greater understandings of other concepts we have already learned. You may find that you retain your current way of thinking, but make sure you understand that change will likely come and test what you believe. Either your beliefs will survive the test or you will change the way you think.

Guard against Taking Offense

The brilliant young rabbi Jesus of Nazareth predicted some future events to His disciples, telling them about the problems they would encounter. He clearly understood the effects of change and the importance of anticipating them, saying, *"'No servant is greater than his master.' If they persecuted me, they will persecute you also. If they obeyed my teaching, they will obey yours also....A time is coming when anyone who kills you will think he is offering a service to God"* (John 15:20, 16:2). He also told them,

> *Nation will rise against nation, and kingdom against kingdom. There will be great earthquakes, famines and pestilences in various places, and fearful events and great signs from heaven. But before all this, they will lay hands on you and persecute you. They will deliver you to... prisons, and you will be brought before kings and governors, and all on account of my name. This will result in your being witnesses to them.... You will be betrayed even by parents, brothers, relatives and friends, and they will put some of you to death. All men will hate you because of me. But not a hair of your head will perish. By standing firm you will gain life.* (Luke 21:10–13; 16–19)

If someone were to stand up in public today and present a list similar to that, he would probably be criticized immediately. Politicians would say, "You're creating hopelessness." Religious leaders might call him a "negative preacher" who "doesn't have any faith." Jesus, however, knew He needed to prepare His disciples for the reality of the changes they would soon experience. He explained to them, *"All this I have told you so that you will not go astray"* (John 16:1). "Astray" has also been translated from the original Greek as *"offended"* (NKJV) and *"stumbling"* (NASB). Jesus repeated to His disciples, *"I have told you this, so that when the time comes you will remember that I warned you"* (John 16:4).

People all over the world today are "offended" and "stumbling" in life by their circumstances and by those whom they blame for those circumstances:

"I lost my house—I am offended by the banking system."

"My husband walked out on me—I'm offended by males."

"I was laid off from my job—I'm offended by corporations."

"I'm getting older—I'm offended by youth."

Jesus warned His disciples in order to protect them from taking offense at their situations and turning away from what is right. He knew how damaging taking offense is to a person's spirit. He prepared them in good times for the tough times. The principle of change assures us that good times won't continue forever, so we must be prepared to avoid the trap of "offense."

Avoid Holding On Too Tightly

Because of this truth, I always remind myself, "Don't hold on to anything too tightly." This concept is found throughout the sacred literature of the Scriptures. Jesus taught, "*Man's life does not consist in the abundance of his possessions*" (Luke 12:15). Life is not measured by what you possess. Why? Because possession can become "recession." In other words, whatever you possess, you obtained from someone or something else. It is not inherent in you, so your possessions can "recede," or be taken away. Therefore, you can't base your personal value on anything you have received because, if you do, then you will lose your value when you no longer have it. In essence, the effects of change will be able to reduce

You can't base your personal value on anything you possess because, if you do, then you will lose your value when you no longer possess it.

you to nothing. So, again, we are protected against change when we don't automatically expect to keep everything we currently have. In this way, we won't be shocked and thrown off course if they go away, either temporarily or permanently.

With the investment fraud and disastrous fiscal policies of various financial institutions in 2008, there were some executives who were enjoying millions one day, only to be arrested and put in jail the next day. Then there was an Illinois governor who was in office one day and impeached and removed from office the next. In addition to any legal difficulties involved in his circumstances, this man was faced with having to find a new job, at the very least. These situations illustrate the fact that it doesn't take long for things to change. Many people who don't realize or accept this fact are so overtaken by change that they start taking drugs and drinking excessively. Some of the perpetrators of financial fraud—or their victims—committed suicide because they felt they'd lost everything when they lost all their money.

Not even a billionaire can count on things to stay the same.

The public image of Donald Trump is one of wealth and success. However, a company that still bears his name filed for bankruptcy protection for its three casinos. Trump, who owns more than 25 percent of the company, played it down, saying his investment in the company was only a small percentage of his net worth. Most people wouldn't have imagined Donald Trump's name occurring in the same sentence as the word *bankruptcy*. Yet no one is immune to change. Likewise, Ed McMahon spent years acquiring wealth and being known as the one who presented millions of dollars to sweepstakes winners. Then he went broke and had to put his possessions up for sale.

Many people are consumed with trying to get to a point where they are wealthy enough to feel secure. Yet if financial troubles and bankruptcy can happen to millionaires and billionaires, as we have seen, then they can happen to anyone.

Most of life's disappointments and stresses come from our trying to keep things the way they are or expecting them to stay the way they are. We can be set free from that pressure by truly understanding that *nothing* on earth lasts forever. *Everything* has a "shelf life." If you have plenty of money now, that may be only temporary. It may not be a permanent state. So, prepare adequately for a time when money will be scarce. Likewise, if you have no money now, things can change tomorrow. Start preparing to build up your finances again.

Two Key Principles for Protection against Change

Let's summarize what we've been discussing with two key principles for protection against change:

1. *The greatest source of disappointment in life is the expectation that things will remain the same.* If you are disappointed, it's because you expected something to occur, and it didn't happen, or because you expected some present situation to always remain the same, and it didn't. People's lives can fall apart when they think that what they're experiencing will never change, only to abruptly learn that the opposite is true.

My doctor told me recently that my blood pressure is perfect. He said, "In your mid-fifties, you have the body of an athlete. You look so healthy; what are you doing?" I replied, "It's not what I'm doing; it's what I'm *not* doing." He said, "What are you not doing?" I said, "Worrying."

How do you reduce your worry level? By lowering your expectation level. Maybe you've been expecting too much from other people—or even yourself. While we want to conduct our lives with excellence, we can't control everything, and we shouldn't try. Trying to control everything that happens to you will overload your body with stress.

The above principle doesn't apply only to situations we would consider negative. It also applies to our general expectations for our lives. Even changes that hold great promise for us often involve various assumptions we've made. For example, suppose your spouse got a job in another country that offered fifteen times more money than he or she is making now. You and your spouse have been struggling to make ends meet, but now that you have this opportunity to move, you suddenly realize how much you love your hometown. The choice is between staying in a comfortable and familiar place but remaining broke, or moving into the unknown but making a good living.

Although such a choice involves more considerations than just money, this scenario highlights one of the challenges of change. You may have expected to live your whole life in the same place where you were born and raised. Yet this might not be God's plan for your life to help you fulfill your purpose. Or, perhaps, through various circumstances, you emigrated from the country of your birth to a different country, and now you find yourself living in an unfamiliar culture. You may ask, "God, why did You bring me here?" He may indicate, "Because your future isn't where you were born—it is where you are now." Expect things to remain the same, and you'll get disappointment.

2. *Our safeguard against disappointment and other negative reactions to change is the anticipation of change.* We must *expect* change. Continually.

To protect yourself from change, acknowledge that anything could happen in the coming months and years. The good news is that God won't allow anything to come into your life that you cannot rise above with His help. I am not afraid of change because I understand that change is a part of life and that I am more durable than it is.

> *God won't allow anything to come into your life that you cannot rise above with His help.*

You must become so stable through anticipating and preparing for change that you can outlast every change. You will keep passing through changes on the way to your purpose, and in the end, you will come out the victor.

> *If you don't like something, change it; if you can't change it,*
> *change the way you think about it.*
> —Mary Engelbreit, artist and entrepreneur

MAXIMIZING CRITICAL CHANGE
Growth, Creativity, and Innovation

The truth is that our finest moments are most likely to occur when we are feeling deeply uncomfortable, unhappy, or unfulfilled. For it is only in such moments, propelled by our discomfort, that we are likely to step out of our ruts and start searching for different ways or truer answers.
—M. Scott Peck, psychiatrist and author of *The Road Less Travelled*

We experience many types of change—some we consider positive, others we perceive as negative; some we regard as minor, others we think of as more significant. Yet there are times when substantial change especially alters our lives or the cultural status quo. This is critical change. The term *critical change* refers to any of the following:

+ a traumatic life event, such as a serious illness or the death of a loved one

+ a turning point that completely changes one's way of life, such as a major relocation or the need to retrain for a new career

+ a radical shift in personal or professional status, such as a divorce or a firing

+ a dire situation that needs to be addressed, such as the effects of a natural disaster or an economic crisis

- an acute challenge to the status quo, such as the survival of an industry or a people

- a crossroads or "zero hour" when a decision or change *must* be made immediately in response to a problem

Almost all the above are considered negative changes. The others reflect times of transition that involve extra stress and demands. Critical change includes both a disruption and a reordering of people's lives. It impels them to deal with new relationships, issues, environments, and circumstances.

Critical Change and Positive Growth

As much as we often wish it weren't, critical change is a part of life. Yet it has a beneficial side, even in the midst of situations in which we experience personal loss. Times of critical change can produce surges of personal growth, creativity, and innovation. If you are experiencing critical challenges—financially, relationally, physically, emotionally—this might become the most fruitful and creative period of your life so far or lead to such a period. While we need to allow ourselves time to grieve our losses, we should also beware of dwelling on those losses rather than discovering how to grow from them.

Periods of personal, community, or national challenge can be times when we undergo the greatest development of maturity, compassion for others, social advancement, and economic development—if we allow the critical change to stretch us and to exercise our innovative qualities. Let your personal motto in such times be *innovation*. Learn to use every situation to maximize your growth and creativity, to cause you to think beyond the norm, so that you can progress in significant ways.

Change: The Greatest Motivator for Progress and Advancement

It is has been said that people initiate personal change only when the pain of remaining the same exceeds the pain of change. To benefit from critical change, we must recognize that it can be the greatest motivator for progress and advancement. Personal, community, financial, and national histories reflect the fact that innovation is often produced by critical change. Critical change is the incubator of improvement.

On an individual level, how many times has a health crisis motivated a person to improve the quality of his or her life? For example, suppose you smoked cigarettes for thirty years, and now you have emphysema. You initiated this critical change in your life, but now it has overwhelmed you, and you have to deal with it. You must stop a lifelong habit. At the same time, you have to learn alternative responses to handling life in order to survive.

On a global level, every great enterprise throughout history was a product of some change in the environment. When the church was stagnant and controlled by tradition, a monk named Martin Luther read the Scriptures and grew uncomfortable with the difference between what he read and what the church was practicing. He helped to initiate the Reformation, a significant departure from the religious tradition of the day, which resulted in the birth of Protestantism.

It is comfort that creates *tradition*. It is discomfort that creates *transformation*.

Let's look at some examples of progress sparked by change in the development of the United States. The creation of the railroad system led to the establishment of towns and cities along the rail routes. Later, as the population of the country grew, so did the incentive to mobilize people. The invention of the car and the construction of a more extensive roadway system followed. The Wright brothers and others developed aviation to further advance the ease of transportation.

Likewise, the development of easier and faster methods of communication were motivated, in part, by the vastness of the United States, which, by 1850, spread from New York to California. How were the East and West coasts—and everywhere in between—to maintain contact in order to keep people connected and to transact business? The expansion of the country led to inventions created under the pressure of necessity or sparked by an opening of opportunity for innovative minds. When mail was transferred by men on horseback, via the Pony Express, it could take weeks, months, or perhaps more than a year for a letter to get from one place to another. The railroads sped up that process. Also, the telegraph allowed communication to occur in seconds, and the telephone provided instant person-to-person communication. The development of the Internet led to e-mail, which is sent in milliseconds.

Progress or development is always motivated by change. What caused John F. Kennedy to announce to Americans in the early 1960s that the country's space program would develop the technology to send astronauts to the moon within a decade? Kennedy's motivation was the pressure of perceived critical change. It was rumored that the Russians were well on their way to attempting such a trip. And he felt that in order to maintain its position in the world, the United States had to be the first country to do so. The Soviet Union's change of technology forced a response in the United States through which NASA's scientists stretched their creative and technical abilities and sent astronauts to the moon in 1969.

Think about the creation of the nuclear bomb during World War II. The Allies and the Axis powers were engaged in a monumental struggle, and both sides sought to invent a weapon that would give them an advantage over their opponents. The critical change of war has often led to the development of more powerful, precise, and deadly weapons.

More recently, scanners in airports had to be developed due to a critical change in the global environment of safety with an increase in hijackings and terrorist acts. That change is still forcing the invention of new technologies. One change produces another change, which is affected by still another change.

In the last two decades of the twentieth century, there was little serious discussion about alternative fuels by officials in government, executives in the corporate world, and the general population. Why? Because, after the gas crisis of the mid-1970s, we got comfortable. There was an adequate supply of gas and oil, prices remained relatively low, and people thought, *Why do we need anything else?* Almost the entire Western world was lulled into a sense of security by the comfort of tradition.

Then, a number of factors converged to bring the issue to the public consciousness, including—but not limited to—tensions between the United States and countries in the Middle East and South America that produce large supplies of oil, the 9-11 attack, the Iraq war, and an increased interest in environmentalism. When gas prices topped four and five dollars late in the first decade of the twenty-first century, interest in alternative fuel sparked. While traditional forms of fuel are still dominant, we are seeing a shift in the general mind-set of people that will continue into the future. Hybrid cars are becoming increasingly popular, with more models offered by car companies each year.

Now, cars that used to be the norm are called "traditional cars." A traditional car is a vehicle that had been accepted as permanent—not in terms of external style but in terms of the type of fuel it ran on and how that fuel was converted into horsepower. But social and political changes are encouraging the development of alternative sources of energy to support all the machinery of life—fueling cars, heating houses, and so forth. People may initially be worried or angry about the advent of innovations, but they and their descendants often reap the benefits of them.

Flying toward the Storm

Somehow, human beings don't seem to grow and innovate as much in good times as in critical times. Again, the average person doesn't know what he is capable of until change affects him or her. I have great confidence in the inner resources of human beings. I believe they are much more powerful than the circumstances confronting the countries and cultures in which they live. In general, the human spirit thrives on finding solutions to chaotic conditions. People often seem to emerge greater, stronger, wiser, and more innovative after going through critical change. We must never despise the power of change to create a better future.

> *The human spirit thrives on finding solutions to chaotic conditions.*

Eagles are the greatest "flying machines" in the world, but we all know that young birds, including eaglets, have to be forced to fly at first. When the mother eagle recognizes that her offspring are too comfortable living amid warm feathers in a snug nest, she begins to rip up the soft, top layers with which the nest is lined: she pulls up the cotton, cloth, and straw to expose the hidden thorns underneath. She instinctively knows that the only way the eaglets will fly is when they are too uncomfortable to remain where they are. They literally need to ascend to a new altitude. As Moses wrote, "[God] *guarded* [His people] *as the apple of his eye, like an eagle that stirs up its nest and hovers over its young, that spreads its wings to catch them and carries them on its pinions*" (Deuteronomy 32:10–11).

Another amazing thing about eagles is that they are the only birds that fly *toward* storms. Every other bird is afraid of storms. Yet eagles spread their wings and use the abnormal wind currents formed by storms in order to soar—giving them an opportunity to rest. They naturally know how to benefit from critical change in their environment.

Do you always run from storms? Or, do you face them, learning how their currents can lift you to higher altitudes and even enable you to rest in the midst of them?

The Benefits of Change

Let's look at several interrelated benefits of change, which we will return to in various ways throughout this book.

1. *Change draws out potential.* Potential is hidden, untapped power, or dormant ability. Normally, ability remains dormant within a person unless he or she is highly motivated internally. People rarely decide on their own to release their true potential. The average person is not motivated enough to take the initiative to tap into his or her unused resources and capabilities but is satisfied with the status quo. Then, change comes and draws out his or her hidden potential. This is why change can be a real benefit to us. Change is vital because it is often the ignition that draws the power from the human battery.

2. *Change challenges potential.* You may feel you have achieved something significant or accomplished something noteworthy—until a change takes place in your life or in your environment that challenges you to go beyond what you previously had been satisfied with. We can become so enamored with what we have already completed that we cease to pursue what we can still accomplish. Change has a way of making us move beyond what used to impress us about ourselves. It shortens our self-congratulatory celebrations and spurs us on to do something greater.

3. *Change pressures potential.* Again, you never know the great things you can accomplish until you *have* to do them. Releasing one's potential usually requires the element of responsibility. Another way of saying this is that *ability* requires *responsibility* in order to be manifested. A change in conditions often forces us to accept duties and obligations that make us dig deeper into the reserves in our capacity.

4. *Change manifests the person behind the potential.* Metaphorically speaking, you don't know what you're carrying inside you until you have to deliver it. When an unexpected event or situation occurs, it can prompt you to manifest a self that people didn't know was in you—that *you* never knew was in you. Unexpected change can help to manifest who you really are. Moreover, we will see that planned change has the same result. When you challenge yourself to implement change in your life toward a better future, you reveal the true self within you.

Therefore, should we curse the chaos in our lives that we don't understand? Or should we seek to understand it so that we may benefit from it?

Success in moving past critical change is determined by one's ability to benefit from it. Develop your capacity to oversee and profit from critical changes in your life and environment. Become an innovator!

> *The world is round and the place which may seem like the end*
> *may also be the beginning.*
> —Ivy Baker Priest, United States Treasurer, 1953–1961

Part 2

THE PURPOSE OF CHANGE

YOUR ONE CONSTANT IN CHANGE

Nothing Is Permanent Except God and His Promises

I the LORD do not change.
—Malachi 3:6

In the popular television series *Lost*, the character Desmond experiences time travel due to an electromagnetic abnormality. Yet this is a different form of time travel. Only his *consciousness* travels from his present self to his past self. Then, the process begins alternating, so that his mind repeatedly travels from present to past and back again. This experience is severely disorienting to him. The continual exchange begins to overload his mind because he has lost his stabilizing sense of continuity in life.

While in the present, Desmond witnesses the same phenomenon happen to another man—whose mind totally rejects what is happening. This man can't maintain a disjointed existence, and he dies of apparent shock. Desmond knows he is headed for the same fate. In a desperate search for a way to save his own life, he seeks out an experimental physics professor. The professor tells him that in order to stop the mental time travel, he has to find someone whom he knows *both* in his past and in his present who can function as his "constant." Desmond successfully identifies his constant, his mind regains its continuity, the time travel ceases, and he is able to continue his life in the present.

In the ever changing world in which we live, many people experience a bit of what Desmond did. We orient our lives based on what we've experienced in the past and the habits and mind-sets we've developed over the years. Sometimes, the mind-set of the past can clash with the present, as well as with the future that is unfolding in our lives, causing our minds to try to reject the changes. Other times, we may be trying to make changes that will move us forward into our preferred futures, only to find the past repeatedly seeming to interfere with our progress.

Whether we are responding to change or creating it, we must have an element in our lives that is permanent and stable—something that transcends the past, the present, and the future. We need to keep our minds and hearts grounded in who we are, where we are going, and the values by which we conduct our lives. We need a "constant," if you will. There is only One who can fill this need.

The Unchangeable One

Our one constant in the midst of change is our Creator God. Despite the fact that everything on earth changes, God declares, *"I the LORD do not change"* (Malachi 3:8). This statement does not imply that God is stagnant, unimaginative, or archaic. Neither does it mean that His modes of operation are unchanging. The opposite is true. Genesis, the first book recorded by Moses, introduces God as Creator. He is the original innovator who initiated the principle of change on earth.

The unchanging nature of the Creator can be compared to the nature of a fundamental principle. Principles are designated as such because they are consistent. The Creator never changes, in the sense that He is invariable in His nature, character, and integrity. His acts may change, but His essential ways never change.

The Scripture says, *"Don't be deceived, my dear brothers. Every good and perfect gift is from above, coming down from the Father of the heavenly lights, who does not change like shifting shadows"* (James 1:16–17).

The writer of the book of Hebrews said, "*Therefore, since we are receiving a kingdom that* **cannot be shaken**, *let us be thankful, and so worship God acceptably with reverence and awe, for our 'God is a consuming fire'*" (Hebrews 12:28–29, emphasis added).

Everything else is changing, but God remains the same. This gives us confidence in the midst of unsettling times.

When Barack Obama was about to be inaugurated president of the United States, an atheist protested against the president-elect placing his right hand on the Bible to swear the oath of office because the atheist said it was against his beliefs, and he considered it to be a violation of his conscience. Some might say he was correct because of their concept of the separation of church and state. Yet, the fact is, the Creator is our only permanency, and ignoring Him or our need for Him in this way would be like removing the only unshakable thing from the office of the presidency. Presidents come and go, but in God, there's no shifting. Ultimately, to have permanency in our changing world, our nations must be built on God, not on people. Our leaders—whether they are presidents, prime ministers, or chairpersons—will fail. But God is the same yesterday, today, and forever. We need to put our faith and trust in Him. We can put no real confidence in anything else, for nothing and no one besides God is completely trustworthy and reliable.

> *The greatest security against the disorientation and disruptions of change is our reliance on the unchanging God.*

Recognizing that God's nature is unchanging is crucial to our understanding of His activities in the lives of human beings and our interpretation of the changes we experience in our generation and world. The greatest security against the disorientation and disruptions of change is our reliance on the unchanging God.

Permanent Promises

God is predictable only in the sense that His nature is unchanging. He is always true to Himself, and He is always true to His word. We can't count on 100 percent truthfulness from any human being, but we can count on God's truthfulness and faithfulness. Moses declared, "*God is not a man, that he should lie"* (Numbers 23:19). Let's look at just a few additional Scriptures that talk about the unchanging nature of God's promises.

Centuries ago, the psalmist wrote, *"Righteous are you, O LORD, and your laws are right....Your promises have been thoroughly tested, and your servant loves them"* (Psalm 119:137, 140). The author of the psalm said, in effect, "I've tested God's promises. Time has tested them. And they are still standing."

Another psalm states, *"Your kingdom is an everlasting kingdom, and your dominion endures through all generations. The LORD is faithful to all his promises and loving toward all he has made"* (Psalm 145:13). Our Creator made us, and He is faithful to all His promises. No matter what changes may come your way, you can depend on Him to fulfill what He promised. If you are meant to have something because God promised it, you will have it, as you receive it in faith and trust in Him to provide it. If you seem to have lost something that God has promised, then you will regain it or its equivalent as you exercise faith and perseverance. You can give thanks that it is on the way.

Paul wrote, *"For no matter how many promises God has made, they are 'Yes' in Christ. And so through him the 'Amen' is spoken by us to the glory of God"* (2 Corinthians 1:20). If God promised it, it's going to happen, regardless of what else occurs. No matter what other people predict about the future, if God has promised something, you can say, "Amen! It is done."

The Promise Paradox

The only two permanent realities in our lives are God and His promises. Yet one of God's own unchanging promises assures us that nothing on earth is permanent!

One reason for this is God's creative nature. If you are a creative person, you're always coming up with new things. That's the nature of God. He is continually refining what He has created, as well as *"doing a new thing"* (Isaiah 43:19). Some people like to think that they have God figured out. They believe that because God doesn't change, He won't do anything differently than what they've already seen Him do. When He brings or allows change in their lives in order to further His purposes for them, they don't know how to react to it. The change unsettles them because they didn't expect it. God Himself doesn't change, but He's always working in our lives—and His work involves transformation. Be assured that God is going to allow something in your life to change.

> *God is always working in our lives—and His work involves transformation.*

If you read the Scriptures, you won't find any account of God performing two miracles in exactly the same way. People often try to make doctrines out of methods God has used in the past instead of realizing that it is His nature, rather than His specific acts, that is permanent. The *results* of those acts may be permanent, but His actions will vary. Why? God is too creative to repeat Himself. His creative nature promotes change. Unless we understand this, we may constantly struggle against the changes He wants to promote in our lives—changes intended to help us to grow and to fulfill the reasons for our existence.

Let me put one note of caution here: This is not to say we should be apathetic and just accept everything that comes into our lives as God's will for us. Rather, we must learn to respond to changing circumstances, keeping in mind His ways and His purposes for us.

This knowledge will enable us to deal with whatever changes come our way. Everything in this world is changeable. Again, we aren't guaranteed that our jobs will last, that our loved ones will always be with us in this life, and so forth. But we do know that we can rely on the unchangeable God and His promises in any critical changes we experience.

I believe in this principle so completely that I've already thought through a number of difficult scenarios that could happen to me or my family and how I might respond to them—anything from losing my home to losing a family member. "Isn't that a lack of faith?" some may ask. No, I have faith in God's promises, and one of His promises is that everything on earth is only for a season. *"There is a time for everything, and a season for every activity under heaven"* (Ecclesiastes 3:1). He has said that we'll go through difficulties in life, but that nothing can separate us from His love. (See Romans 8:35–39.) I prepare for any eventuality because, as we noted earlier, Jesus warned His disciples that they would experience difficult times, and He said, in effect, "I told you these things so you won't be offended." Critical change won't offend me to the point of questioning God and His love, because I know that He has warned us about it. Once, when Jesus was describing God's overall plan for those who believe in Him, He said, *"If it were not so, I would have told you"* (John 14:2). God keeps His Word. He tells us how things are. He comforts us, but He doesn't give us false promises. If things were any different, He would have told us. He's Someone whom we can count on completely to tell us the truth and to prepare us to handle it.

Many people in Western society have been led to believe that nothing they value in their lives should change, unless it changes by increasing in size or worth. Therefore, they think they will always have their houses, have full bank accounts, have money for expensive vacations and electronics, and so forth. Increasingly, many people expect that they should automatically have such things, regardless of whether they work for them. The good life should be guaranteed, according to them, because "it's the American dream," or for other reasons.

A similar attitude is being taught by some within the Christian church. People are told that God wants them to be successful, so they can always expect "the good life." This theology, however, has produced believers who cannot handle change. Instead of being taught the permanency of God's nature and character, they have been taught that God promises the permanency of *things*. In other words, they hear that if they have faith, they can build up wealth and happiness and keep things this way for the rest of their lives.

Certainly, we should have faith in God's promises. Yet He never guarantees there won't be times when we'll have to hold on to His promises no matter what things appear to be, and against all odds. In the Scriptures, people who were called by God to further His purposes and gain His blessings often lost things before they received something better.

Abraham had to leave his country and family in order to receive a great blessing from God. Moreover, he and his wife, Sarah, had to forgo having a child in their youth in order to receive a miracle child in their old age. This delay was the result of God's purpose, not a lack of faith. Joseph lost seemingly everything: the experience of his father's favor, his boyhood home, and his family inheritance—when his brothers sold him into slavery. Then, he was falsely accused and forgotten in jail for years before he was promoted to the role of Pharaoh's right-hand man in Egypt. Similarly, the changes and transitions that come our way are part of the process, and we must hold firmly to God's nature and purposes in the midst of them so that we can arrive safely at the destination He intended. Many people have forfeited their rewards because they've questioned God's love or even their own faith.

Again, life is not meant to continue on the way it always has been. It is meant to become the way it's supposed to be *next*. So, we need to try our best to learn God's purposes for us, to ask Him to guide us, and to discern what is next. In this way, we will not become overwhelmed by the present on our way to the future. To us, life is unpredictable. To God, life is always moving toward the fulfillment of His ultimate purposes.

> *Life is not meant to continue on the way it always has been. It is meant to become the way it's supposed to be* **next.**

Preparing our hearts and minds for any eventuality will help take the sting out of change. And we must remember that God is with us in all the changes we experience. He prepares us for change, and He's never surprised by it. For example, we all know that death is inevitable. That is the ultimate critical change we will experience. But Jesus has already conquered death for us. While still on earth, He knew that His death on our behalf was coming, and He prepared Himself for it. In this sense, He conquered death even before He died. The battle was won in His mind and heart when He said to God the Father, "*Not my will, but yours be done*" (Luke 22:42). And so, the Scriptures say, "*Where, O death, is your victory? Where, O death, is your sting?*" (1 Corinthians 15:55). We know that death still exists for the time being. But it's like a bee that has lost its sting. While we will all have to die, Jesus has already provided for that change. He has gone before us in death, and we will follow Him into resurrection if we trust in Him. And so, we can live with the understanding that we must prepare for the inevitability of death while still having the eternal, unchangeable hope of resurrection with Christ.

God wants us to live with a clear understanding of the nature of change in our lives so that we'll be spared the stress of fighting against it. Again, everything has a season; nothing is permanent—except God and His promises. That statement goes two ways. It's not only the "good" things that are temporary or seasonal. Whatever difficulty you are going through is also only for a season. Whatever is happening to you will not last.

God Is Doing "A New Thing"

Our Creator knows that it is sometimes difficult for us to accept the changes He is making in our lives. He knows that we often expect things to remain the same, and that we get used to Him working in a certain way. So, He gave us some encouragement in the book of the prophet Isaiah: *"Forget the former things; do not dwell on the past. See, I am doing a new thing! Now it springs up; do you not perceive it?"* (Isaiah 43:18–19). To "see" refers to observing. Sometimes, we don't recognize what's happening to us, around us, and in us. God says, "Open your eyes and study your environment. What do you perceive?"

Do you perceive the new things God is doing in your life? Do you perceive the new things God is doing in your life? Stay in touch with Him through prayer and reading His Word so you won't become overwhelmed by change in your life. Stay close to Him, because His character doesn't change. David, the poet-warrior-king, wrote, *"Therefore we will not fear, though the earth give way and the mountains fall into the heart of the sea"* (Psalm 46:2). How could he say that? Because he trusted in God as his *"strong tower"* (Psalm 61:3) and his *"rock"* (Psalm 18:2).

Is the Creator God Your Constant?

Do you know your "Constant"? You must rely on the Unchangeable One in the midst of change to keep yourself stable in times of transition and upheaval. Again, seek to understand and interpret the changes in your life so that they don't shake you. Instead, use them to move forward in God's purposes for your life. You may even experience a time when there are so many changes that you begin to wonder, *Is God against me?* This is the time to remember that He allows change to come in order to fulfill His purposes in us and through us. These vital principles of change will help see you through:

1. Nothing is permanent except God and His promises.

2. God's character and nature are unchanging.

3. God promises us that nothing on earth is permanent.

4. God uses change to advance His purposes in our lives.

The eternal God is your refuge, and underneath are the everlasting arms.
—Deuteronomy 33:27

THE NATURE AND CHARACTERISTICS OF SEASONS
Change Is Built into Creation

The one unchangeable certainty is that nothing is certain or unchangeable.
—John F. Kennedy

God is not only unchangeable, but He is also eternal. The Scriptures record that the patriarch Abraham *"called upon the name of the LORD, the Eternal God"* (Genesis 21:33). Eternity is not ruled by time. God exists outside of time, although He interacts with human beings and human affairs within the realm of time.

Our world functions in time because God created it that way. The purpose of time is clearly stated in the biblical account of His creation of the world: *"And God said, 'Let there be lights in the expanse of the sky to separate the day from the night, and let them serve as signs to mark seasons and days and years'"* (Genesis 1:14, emphasis added). The term *"seasons"* denotes change. The sun and other stars in the sky serve as signs to mark seasons and days and years. That's why we measure days and nights, which become months, which become years, which become decades, which become centuries, which become millennia.

In essence, the creation of time was the original source of change in our world. Some of the change we experience today is a result of evil acts perpetrated by others. Sin entered the world when humanity rebelled against God and went its own way. Yet change itself is not a result of the fall of humanity. It is built into creation.

Change and Seasons

Time produces change, and everything that exists and functions within time inevitably experiences change. King Solomon stated in one of his books of wisdom,

> *To everything there is a season, a time for every purpose under heaven.*
> (Ecclesiastes 3:1 NKJV)

These words capture the spirit of change that is inherent in time: everything is "seasonal," or functions in a limited time frame. They also communicate the following principles, which are the foundation for what we have been discussing. In the first few chapters, we looked at the effects of change, but these principles explain *why* change is an inevitable factor in our lives.

1. Everything that is created—everything that is below the invisible, eternal realm of God—exists in time.

2. Everything that exists in time has a purpose, and each of these purposes has a season for its fulfillment.

3. God's purposes and activities within time are designed for seasons, which in turn require change.

Because we live in a world governed by time, we live according to seasons, and our lives are subject to change. Change is the essence of our experience of life.

When I was a teenager, I came to understand the function of seasons—physical, personal, spiritual, and so forth—and my attitude toward life was totally transformed. It happened as I was reading and thinking about the statement by Solomon that we looked at above: *"To everything there is a season, a time for every purpose under heaven"* (Ecclesiastes 3:1 NKJV).

The musical group The Byrds used these same words of Solomon in one of their songs, "Turn, Turn, Turn!" Many people have heard the song and even sung the lyrics—but its meaning doesn't really register with them. To them, it's a catchy tune with easy words. However, I believe that if more people truly realized what these words meant, there would be less self-imposed destruction through suicide, alcoholism, drugs, pornography, and other means of escape from the difficulties of life. If we *know* that everything in life is only for a season—and I believe this has to be an individual revelation for each person—then we're relieved of the pressure of trying to keep everything the way it has been. It takes some of the shock out of life when we experience situations that otherwise would lead us to bewildering grief, disappointment, and fear. The average person still expects life to be one long summer. People forget that life brings winters and autumns and springs, too.

I look at seasons as God's promise of change. First, physical seasons were created by God to mark time and to remind us that, on earth, life is full of changes. Second, personal and spiritual seasons in our lives are designed to move us toward His purposes. Seasons bring us hope and the assurance of progress.

> *Personal and spiritual seasons in our lives are designed to move us toward God's purposes.*

Let's take a closer look at what God's Word teaches about seasons so that we can more completely apply the principles of change in our lives. The word *season* is often used to define change that is not a short-term event but rather an extended period of transition.

The Promise of Change

In various places in His Word, God the Creator promises the existence of seasons. These passages teach us more about His ways and the nature of change. Let's explore a few of them.

Seedtime and Harvest

"As long as the earth endures, seedtime and harvest, cold and heat, summer and winter, day and night will never cease" (Genesis 8:22). This passage

assures us that *"as long as the earth endures,"* there will be seasons. Since we're all still here, living on earth, we need to settle into the pattern that God has established for this world and know that we will experience seasons of change.

Some of you are in the midst of "seedtime." You're in a period when you're investing yourself in certain aspects of your life. You are not at a place where you're seeing visible results because it's still time for you to plant. Wait a while. The harvest is coming. Or, perhaps you are currently experiencing "harvest." Everything you've worked for and everything you need is flowing in. Enjoy the harvest. At the same time, prepare for the off-season, when you will transition to a new period of sowing seed.

Some of you are in the "winter" season, so the promise of change sounds especially good to you. You can't wait for the snow to melt and the grass to turn green in your life again. Others of you are in the midst of "summer" right now; things are going well, and you have few worries. When we are in the middle of summer, we can tend to look down on those who are in winter, forgetting our own past winters or the fact that other winters will come into our lives. This is why, as I said earlier, seasons are the great equalizer. Some of us may stay longer in certain seasons than others seem to, but at some point, our seasons will change. Let's learn to recognize each season and how people experience it so that we can have understanding hearts toward others.

Some of you are in "night" right now. Life seems confusing or even hopeless. You can't seem to see very far into the future, and what you do see is dim. God assures you, "Yes, night is part of what you will experience, but remember that after every night, there's day." *"Weeping may endure for a night, but joy comes in the morning"* (Psalm 30:5 NKJV).

People who understand the principles of change handle changing seasons without wavering in their purposes because they know the Unchangeable One. They understand that as long as they put their faith in Him, they, too, will remain steady.

In essence, God is telling us through the Scriptures, "Settle down. If it's night in your life right now, don't panic. Day is on the way. If it feels like winter in your finances or in your marriage, spring will come." Sometimes, we tend to remember only certain of God's promises, such as "I will bless you" and "I will heal you." Yes, He will bless us, but He also says we will experience night. He will heal us, but there may also be wintertimes.

To Everything There Is *Only* a Season

Let's return to one of my favorite sayings of King Solomon, which reinforces the message of the above passage from Genesis: *"There is a time for everything, and a season for every activity under heaven"* (Ecclesiastes 3:1). We could read this as, "To everything, there is a season, and to every purpose, there is a time."

I understand this statement to signify, "To everything, there is *only* a season." Since there's a time for everything, then things won't necessarily last as long as we think they're going to. If we wait long enough, things will change again. Change moves us closer to God's purposes for our lives—if we allow it to.

Change moves us closer to God's purposes for our lives—if we allow it to.

Let's look at the illustration of employment again. There's a time for you to be working at the job you currently have. In your mind, this may seem like a lifetime career. Yet the Creator may be saying, "You don't know how long this season is going to last." When the time comes to leave, the company may call it a layoff, a downsizing, or even a firing, but God calls it "moving on." The perspective you will have depends on how you understand life and the nature of change.

Again, we must settle the truth in our minds and hearts that everything is seasonal. We have to stop looking at life from just one standpoint. For example, some of you used to be managers and executives at corporations; you had your own private parking spots near the front door. You never used to interact with the employees who rode the bus and went to their jobs through the warehouse entrance. Now, you've been laid off or fired, and it is you who are riding the bus to work. Be thankful to God for whatever you have right now. Because nothing is permanent. Learn to be grateful when you have just a little. You have to stay humble. No matter what happens in your life, let your attitude be, "Thank You for everything, Lord." Then, wait patiently until your season changes for the better.

Times, Seasons, and Rulers

"Praise be to the name of God for ever and ever; wisdom and power are his. He changes times and seasons; he sets up kings and deposes them" (Daniel 2:20–21). God *changes* times and seasons. I take this not just literally, but also figuratively. God is in charge of the universe, and He is working in the lives of men and women in order to fulfill His purposes. If He wants to create a new tide in the ebb and flow of human history, He will do so. If He decides to change the leadership of a nation, He will do so. What the Bible says about change, therefore, is more important than what the news broadcasts are saying, because God is in control. We shouldn't put our ultimate trust in any person—or anything—but God.

Showers of Blessing in Season

"I will bless them and the places surrounding my hill. I will send down showers in season; there will be showers of blessing" (Ezekiel 34:26). Notice that *"showers of blessing"* come in seasons. We must understand that when the blessings start coming, that is not a permanent condition. When the showers stop, will your faith remain intact? Or will you think God is no longer coming through for you? We may think that God has forgotten us, but we're only experiencing a season.

Just as I was a teenager when I first read the wisdom of Solomon, I was a teenager when I first read the above verse. My parents had taught my brothers and sisters and me how to read the Bible and memorize Scripture passages. One of the first chapters of the Bible they made us memorize was Psalm 1, which includes these verses:

> *Blessed is the man who does not walk in the counsel of the wicked or stand in the way of sinners or sit in the seat of mockers. But his delight is in the law of the LORD, and on his law he meditates day and night. He is like a tree planted by streams of water, which yields its fruit in season and whose leaf does not wither. Whatever he does prospers.*
>
> (Psalm 1:1–3)

"In season." Just as there will be showers in season, there will be particular seasons that bring forth fruit. As we talked about earlier, you may

be working hard but not seeing any results. That's just a normal part of the season. You will bring forth your fruit in its time.

"*Whose leaf does not wither.*" Leaves have an important function, even though they are not the fruit. Leaves are a sign that the tree is alive and healthy enough to bear fruit. If your life is currently manifesting "leaves," it means your "roots," or your faith, are still grounded. You are drawing living water from your Creator that will bear rich fruit in the future. This is the time to trust in Him, to plan hard, and to work diligently. Soon, a season will come when you can "feed" others through the fruit that you bear.

"*Whatever he does prospers.*" This is the harvest season—a time of fruitfulness and abundant prosperity. We will be blessed "*in season.*"

The Meaning of Seasons and Times

The following descriptions summarize the meaning of seasons and times for us:

- *Change* and *Temporary Conditions:* Natural rhythms exist all around us. There are seasons in nature, with corresponding changes in the weather, and seasons in our bodies. There are seasons in our personal lives and seasons within the changing tides of human history. The very nature of seasons implies change. Seasons indicate the nonpermanent nature of conditions in time and assure us that nothing remains the same.

- *Transition* and *Convergence:* Changing seasons denote transitions in time, as well as points of convergence where two seasons meet.

- *Difference:* Seasons involve the replacement of one environment or condition with another different from itself.

- *Time period:* The reality of seasons suggests that present conditions exist within the parameters of a finite time span.

Inherent Characteristics of God-Ordained Seasons

Finally, if we are to oversee change in our personal lives, as well as enter into the change God is orchestrating in the world at large, we must acknowledge the following inherent characteristics of God-ordained seasons.

Generational Seasons Are Natural

I believe that when a generation of people experiences a new societal or spiritual season (these two may be connected), it is a natural fulfillment of the progression of God's purpose in the world. Because these changes are natural, the effects are felt first in people's hearts, and then they are seen in people's actions. For example, in the Introduction, I talked about what I see as the current worldwide shift in focus from industrialized nations to Third World countries and oppressed peoples. This shift began all over the world at the same time. God's Spirit started to prepare people of the Third World for leadership roles in the twenty-first century. I have visited more than fifty nations and discovered the same phenomenon—a sudden sense of confidence, destiny, responsibility, and leadership in the hearts of thousands of unsung leaders. I will discuss this trend in more detail in the next chapter.

Concurrently, I have discovered a change in the hearts of many leaders in industrialized nations who have held the reins of leadership, influence, and authority for decades. Many of them have admitted that they felt this shift in responsibility was taking place and have announced it publicly.

God-Ordained Seasons Cannot Be Stopped, Resisted, or Controlled

Recognizing that God-ordained seasons cannot be resisted is vital to our response to them. Nothing can stop a season that is divinely ordered. The power that propels such a season is beyond our comprehension. Even though God has created each of us with a free will, we are still subject to His sovereign purposes for the world.

Some have tried to direct or control a providential move of God. Others have tried to take credit for it and label the change as a personal accomplishment. But the Creator will not allow it. His new season will not be controlled. It won't be the trophy of any group, individual, or organization. It is *His* change.

Many are the plans in a man's heart, but it is the Lord's purpose that prevails. (Proverbs 19:21)

No matter what our personal desires, wishes, or attitudes may be, we cannot control an unfolding season of divine destiny. Just as we can't stop winter from coming after autumn, we can't prevent a season of God's purpose, no matter how much we may become angry, pray, or propose plans for doing so. The change is inevitable. It has arrived in the fullness of time. The beginning and ending of a season are not determined by man but by God's sovereign agenda.

The LORD Almighty has purposed, and who can thwart him?

(Isaiah 14:27)

God-Given Seasons Do Not Consider Human Status

Someone opposing a new season of God may be intelligent or powerful in the eyes of the world, such as a top-notch lawyer, a billionaire businessman, a nationally known pastor, a Nobel Prize-winning scientist, a Pulitzer prize-winning author, a country's leader, or an international banker. Yet God-given seasons do not take into consideration human status. They are not impressed by titles, accomplishments, or positions. Rather, they require acceptance of, and cooperation with, the "new thing" that God is doing.

Some people see their present positions and even their convictions threatened by a new God-ordained season. They want to dictate and manipulate the sovereign will of the Creator. Consequently, they may predict "movements of God" that are contrary to what He is actually doing within a nation or around the world. Yet, again, such seasons are controlled by God, and they do not require the permission of any group of apparently distinguished, influential leaders in order to be initiated. All of us are only players in a brief portion of history. As such, we should be committed to fulfilling our own God-given assignments in our soon-to-be-fading generations. We must realize that the demise of a season and the arrival of a new one does not need our blessing; it contains its own blessing.

We should be committed to fulfilling our own God-given assignments in our generations.

However, we must also realize that the beginning of a new season or generation does not negate the roles we have played in our own seasons and generations, under God's direction. "*God is not unjust; he will not forget your work and the love you have shown him as you have helped his people and continue to help them*" (Hebrews 6:10).

Moses was honored, as was his successor, Joshua.

Elijah was honored, was his successor, Elisha.

Paul was honored, as was his "*true son in the faith,*" Timothy (1 Timothy 1:2).

We are not "set aside" by God—unless we actively work against Him. We will receive our reward as we are faithful to follow His purposes in our changing times.

Each new season grows from the leftovers from the past. That is the essence of change, and change is the basic law.
—Hal Borland, journalist and author

WORLDWIDE TIDES OF CHANGE
Ten Areas Converging to Transform Our World

Wherever we are, it is but a stage on the way to somewhere else, and whatever we do, however well we do it, it is only a preparation to do something else that shall be different.
—Robert Louis Stevenson, author

I wrote in the preface to this book that we are living in a time when there is a convergence of worldwide changes that is creating a transitional tide in human history. I defined *historic convergence* as a strategic period of history when major events occur, bringing with them momentous transformations in social, economic, political, and spiritual conditions.

Times of shifting periodically occur in societies. These lead to, for example, changes in the way governments or economies function. Yet a historic convergence goes deeper and wider than these parameters. Transitional tides incorporate trends that have been building and manifesting for some time and that are bringing about a significant transformation to the world as it has been known up to that point.

The Generational Progression of Humankind

Earlier, I discussed the relationship between purpose, times, and seasons. The world of change we're experiencing today can be understood in the context of the unfolding of God's ultimate will for the earth. I believe there is a providential order in the generational progression of humankind. Understanding the principles and benefits of change, especially in relation to seasons and times, is critical if we are to interpret the activities of God in our generation.

Some of the change we're experiencing around the world is motivated by the designs of evil men and involves much pain in people's lives. Therefore, it is important to understand that, in working out His purposes, God does not *cause* this evil. Rather, He *uses* all things—both the good and the bad—for the purpose of moving the world toward His ultimate intent. This is why Joseph could say to his brothers, who had sold him into slavery and told his father that he was dead, *"Don't be afraid. Am I in the place of God? You intended to harm me, but God intended it for good to accomplish what is now being done, the saving of many lives"* (Genesis 50:19–20).

Continuing Trends

In this chapter, we will look at ten defining areas of life that are converging to bring about a transitional tide in human history. Responding rather than reacting to these momentous changes is crucial for us, no matter where we live on the globe, in order to reap the benefits of them and to fulfill our God-given purposes. Fifteen to twenty years ago, I recognized the signs of several of these areas of change, and I began speaking about them in conferences and elsewhere in order to help people prepare for them. These include the increased influence of China on the world scene and the rise of leadership in various Third World nations.

Before we look at these specific areas, however, let us take an overview of the general spheres of life in which these transitions are occurring, as well as some of their implications.

Spheres of Transition

1. *Generational Transition:* Many founders and leaders of influential organizations, institutions, religious ministries, and national governments are entering the twilight of their lives. Their departure is making way for the emergence and ascension of new leadership from younger generations.

You may be at a point in life when you are handing over the leadership of a political body, a community organization, a business, a ministry, or even a family. Or, you may be at a place where the reins of leadership are being handed to you. How will you handle this change? Do you find yourself reacting or responding to it? Your response to generational transition is vital to carrying forward God's work in the world.

2. *Political Transition:* The international balance of power is shifting from the one known by previous generations. Global political power seems to be moving from the West to the East and from the north to the south. A world dominated by the Cold War and superpower standoffs has transformed into a realignment of nations and the emergence of international terrorism. The United States is no longer considered the sole policeman in global affairs. The increased role of the United Nations in mediating international disputes and addressing social concerns is a part of this complex, new political world we are entering. The emergence of a multiplicity of small and large states to important positions in the world equation also demands attention.

You may be living in a country in which political power is declining or is taking on a new form. Or, you may be living in a nation that is coming into increased influence and power in the world. Perhaps your country still maintains weight in the international community or is struggling for some kind of recognition. How will you address the political atmosphere in the world today and in your home country? Seeking to understand the emerging political world and the ways in which God is working in this realm is also crucial to being a participant in His purposes at this time.

3. *Economic Transition:* International finance has caused the economies of the world's nations to become more closely intertwined than at any other time in history. The economic aftershocks of the 2008 stock market crisis and its ongoing fluctuations, the international recession, and the growing unemployment rates have rocked nations and worldwide markets. The

longevity and full impact of these factors is still unknown. The opening of China politically and economically, and the rise of the economies in other Asian countries, as well as in various South American, Central American, and African nations, have contributed to a more complex marketing environment in international affairs. Moreover, national and international terrorism has the potential to compromise the economic and social stability of nations.

How will you relate to the economic reality of today's world? While some people may try to deny or ignore it, responding to it wisely and constructively as you ultimately trust in God for your provision will enable you to benefit during our complex and uncertain economic times.

4. *Religious Transition:* Nations long considered Christian strongholds have seen a decline in church affiliation and attendance. The expansion of Eastern, mystic religions, such as Hinduism and Buddhism, and the rise of Islam, are important components in this new equation. The emigration of African, Eastern, and Middle Eastern peoples to European nations and the United States is also contributing to this changing climate.

Do you have a realistic view of shifting religious affiliations and the growth of religions in the world? Knowing the facts will enable you to understand the state of the world today and give you insight into the natures of some of the cultural changes and clashes that are occurring. This knowledge is vital to having an informed view of the world and your role in it.

5. *Spiritual Transition:* It is necessary to make a distinction between religious and spiritual transition in the world because spiritual transition involves direct divine activity, whereas religious transition may be the result of mere human activity. The spiritual transition seems to be from north to south, from old to young, from the known to the unknown, and from the expected to the unexpected.

Many Third World countries are developing their own spiritual leaders and effective ministries. The church in the West needs new attitudes and positions with regard to its relationship to the church in Third World environments. Major spiritual revival around the globe seems to be focused in developing nations, and this trend appears to be continuing. I believe God is moving among nations, producing a "spiritual sense of nationalism."

By this, I mean a sense of responsibility for praying for and working toward the salvation of their people.

A knowledge of the activity of God's Spirit is vital to your participation in His work in the hearts of men, women, and children around the world. Do you understand the ways in which He is drawing people to Himself in various nations? In your own nation?

6. *Social and Cultural Transition:* In recent years, the social infrastructure of many nations has been transformed by increased access to formal education and long-distance educational programs, the explosion of the information age, and the expansion of travel. These factors have produced more internationally educated citizens. The average individual of today's world is much more sophisticated and knowledgeable about the world than the average individual of fifty years ago.

In addition, the ease of global transportation in our fast-shrinking world has produced a mobile world population. This mobility has diluted the distinction and isolation between cultures and nations of the earth. The exportation of Western culture through television, movies, and international trade is also changing family and social dynamics in nations. The world has truly become a "global village."

How will you respond to the social and cultural transitions taking place in the world today? Are you comfortable interacting with other cultures? How much do you know about groups of people who are different from you—whether in your own nation or in another nation? As you seek to be part of God's purposes for the world today, will you ignore or accept the reality of cultural change?

These are a few of the major spheres of life in which transition is taking place. Reading about them may make you excited or hopeful. Or, it may make you nervous or worried. Yet, even in the midst of changes that seem confusing, inconvenient, or destructive, we can trust God to be working in us and through us. As Paul wrote, "*God has not given us a spirit of fear, but of power and of love and of a sound mind*" (2 Timothy 1:7 NKJV). He will give us strength and wisdom in all the changes

God will give us strength and wisdom in all the changes we experience in our world.

we experience in our world. He will enable *us* to be world changers in the midst of our changing world.

A Historic Convergence of Ten Major Areas of Life

What are some defining aspects of life that are converging to transform our world into something distinct from the recent past? Below are ten major areas of transformation, many of which you will recognize as influencing and characterizing your everyday life.

These ten areas are complex, so what follows just scratches the surface of what is occurring. Many other factors are involved. However, this summary will give you a general idea of the world in which we're living and the world that is emerging. We should also keep in mind that these areas are often interrelated. For instance, globalization, communication, mobilization, technology, and political transformation all have an effect on economic change.

The times in which we're living may be summarized as the age of...

1. Globalization
2. Information
3. Communication
4. Mobilization
5. Cultural Diversification
6. Mergers and Networking
7. Longevity of Life
8. Technology
9. Political and Religious Transition
10. Rapid Transformation

The Age of Globalization

By "The Age of Globalization," I am referring to economic markets and competition, as well as to the social impact of the international economy on people's lives.

Global economics are in a state of change, producing far-reaching repercussions. The financial crisis of 2008 and 2009 has punctuated and accelerated this change. Its long-term implications have yet to be assessed. What is abundantly clear is that economic interdependence is now a reality in our world. In addition, we are seeing a shift from local to national markets and from national to global markets.

At the same time, the growth of some developing nations has produced stronger economic environments for them, resulting in stronger money markets. This economic change also includes the improved management of resources in countries where effective management skills had been lacking. However, the financial downturn of 2008 and 2009 is negatively impacting the level of growth in developing nations such as Nigeria, the largest exporter of oil on the African continent. Again, it is too early to tell how this will impact these countries in the long run.

I remember vividly when the reality of globalization first sank in for me. It was at the time when the Japanese were really expanding their trade markets and becoming very wealthy as they dominated world exports. I was in Los Angeles, California, for a speaking engagement, and I was riding in a taxi. As I looked up at one of the skyscrapers, I told my driver, "That's a beautiful building," and he said, "Yeah, that's not ours." I said, "What do you mean?" He said, "The Japanese just bought it." *The Japanese bought that huge building right in the middle of downtown Los Angeles?* I thought.

Then I went to Seattle, Washington, and noticed another especially impressive skyscraper while I as riding in a taxi. I told the driver, "That's a beautiful building," and he said, "The Japanese just bought it." I went to Omaha, Nebraska, to speak, and I commented on one of the buildings there to my driver. He said, "The Japanese just bought it." I thought, *The Japanese are buying up American real estate. What's going on here?*

Such foreign acquisition of real estate in America may seem more common today, but at the time, it was especially significant as an indication of an emerging economic trend. Now, China is the country people are watching as it grows economically and influentially in the world.

What does "The Age of Globalization" mean for you? It impacts the goods your nation sells in world markets, and the goods you buy through

Are you prepared to respond to change with practical strategies and plans?

international trade. It affects the balance of trade in the world and the trade surplus or deficit of your nation. It may also impact your livelihood. Suppose you are a businessperson who used to compete with the company across the street or across the state. Now, you may be competing for business with someone across the world. Are you prepared to respond to that change with practical strategies and plans?

The Age of Information

Desiderius Erasmus was a Dutch scholar who died in the sixteenth century. In his approximately seventy years of life, he was reputedly the last person ever to have been able to read everything (still preserved) that had been written up to his lifetime. After that, recorded information became too great for anyone to accomplish that feat!

Yet today, more information, covering more topics, is available to more people than at any other time in history. It is accessible through books (print and electronic), magazines, television, radio, library collections, courses on DVD, college and university programs, business and technical schools, community classes, lectures, computer programs, the Internet, online courses, and the list goes on. This is the age of twenty-four-hour news and information bombardment.

What does "The Age of Information" mean for you? On the one hand, you have a remarkable opportunity to educate yourself and enjoy a wide exposure to knowledge, news, the arts, and so forth. On the other hand, you will need discernment. For example, although a wide variety of information is available through the Internet, it cannot always be verified as accurate. In addition, with the amount of information coming at us in any given day through a variety of sources, we need to learn to filter it, or it could easily become too distracting or overwhelming. Time needed to focus on important tasks and projects could be eaten away. We may feel increased demands on us to respond to each news item or crisis that comes our way, when only so much can be dealt with effectively by one person. In response to this age of information, multitasking and obtaining knowledge, resources, and entertainment through a variety of media is becoming a way of life for many people. As this trend continues, the benefits of accomplishing a greater number of tasks will need to be balanced with the ability to focus and explore topics in detail. Depth and complexity—through which balanced perspectives and viable solutions are acquired—are often lost in our information age.

The Age of Communication

In the very last decade of the eighteenth century, the telegraph was developed, and in the nineteenth century, the telephone was invented. In the twentieth century, new forms of communication exploded. But consider this: during the time of the Roman empire, when someone wanted to send a message to a military commander, the message had to be delivered by a courier on horseback—or on foot. The same thing was true up until the Revolutionary War in America. That was how General George Washington received his messages. No new innovations for communicating quickly or efficiently were invented or employed during that entire time period—or earlier. This gives us a little perspective on how much change new communication methods have brought to our world and how rapidly they are being developed and refined.

We now live in a time when there is not only abundant information but also widespread dissemination of information in many forms. "The Age of Communication" is about more than the availability of information. It is about connecting people—often instantaneously—all over the world. It's about constant communication through cell phones, BlackBerries, Twitter, and other technology. It is about increased markets and business. It is about the diffusion of ideas and the reporting of events worldwide. The following are some characteristics and results of this trend.

Increased speed: Fewer people are using regular or "snail" mail if they can send e-mail. While people used to receive letters in two or three days, now they receive e-mail in milliseconds. This is extremely convenient, but it also places new demands on us because businesses, family members, and friends now want us to respond immediately. It can be overwhelming to try to keep up with this correspondence. (How many e-mails come to your in-box each day?)

In a similar way, whereas people used to keep in touch with others less regularly—possibly through limited phone calls in the evenings or through cards or letters—now, people call each other frequently throughout the day just to ask, "What are you doing right now?" Increased connection both encourages relationships and puts pressure on people to remain in constant contact with others while also working and carrying on the business of life.

Increased speed also refers to the rapidity with which we can send packages around the world, our ability to sign contracts and complete applications online, and similar conveniences.

Increased insecurity: Through long-distance communication, some companies are now hiring people overseas to work for them. This can bring a sense of insecurity in the workplace for a number of people. For example, telemarketing and computer technical assistance are often outsourced. Employees in the United States may lose their jobs to workers in Asia who are hired to do their jobs instead. To use another illustration, perhaps you are a freelance graphic artist who used to have a comfortable client base in your community. Now, many companies are having their graphic arts work done by freelance artists who work online—and can live anywhere in the world. Unless you are also able to develop a Web site and work online, your chosen profession may be in jeopardy. Therefore, the Age of Communication can bring increased insecurity as well as convenience for many people.

Bigger markets with greater access and fewer barriers: Both large and small businesses can market to customers in countries around the world, yielding higher revenues. They can sell their products online to people almost anywhere and at any time. Likewise, individual consumers can buy products online from almost anywhere and at any time. In addition to businesses, organizations can connect to others around the world with fewer cultural and logistical barriers.

The Age of Mobilization

This is an age of increased mobilization, although aspects of mobility are being hampered by certain challenges. On the one hand, travel to other countries is more accessible and convenient, and more people have the resources to take such trips. People also have increased access to personal transportation. For example, the number of car sales in the developing country of China has significantly increased. Affordable, fuel-efficient, and environmentally friendly cars are being produced. National and international trade promotes the quick and efficient transportation of goods around the world.

On the other hand, air travel is vulnerable due to many airlines' troubles with solvency. When terrorist acts and threats involving airplanes have occurred, such as 9-11, air traffic has dropped dramatically—creating staggering financial losses for airlines. Increased fuel costs and other factors have caused a reduction in the number of flights available. Moreover, mass transportation—such as buses—is often cut back in cities that are having financial difficulties.

Still, developments like ultrafast train networks, such as the Alta Velocidad Espanola (AVE) being built in Spain, are changing the cultural—and sometimes physical—landscapes in some nations. The *Wall Street Journal* reported,

> Many Spaniards are fiercely attached to their home regions and studies show they are unusually reluctant to live or even travel elsewhere. But those centuries-old habits are starting to change....
>
> "We Spaniards didn't used to move around much," says Jose Maria Menendez, who heads the civil engineering department at the University of Castilla-La Mancha.... "The AVE has radically changed this generation's attitude to travel."[1]

"The Age of Mobilization," therefore, is a trend to keep watching closely. While there will always be a market for the mobilization of people and products, less demand for travel worldwide may put more emphasis on communication. People may opt to connect through electronic means— teleconferencing for business purposes, for example—rather than spend the time and money for travel.

What does the Age of Mobilization mean for you? It provides you the opportunity to visit other countries and cultures. If you are a businessperson, it enables you to market to areas of the world you may never have dreamed of reaching. If you have a ministry or organization that desires to improve the lives of others overseas, it gives you easier access to other nations and the ability to bring resources and helping hands to those areas. In general, it gives more people the freedom to go where they want to, when they want to.

The Age of Cultural Diversification

"The Age of Cultural Diversification" is connecting people, cultures, and nations. Cultures that were once foreign to one other are now familiar with one another. In addition, the cultural makeup within countries is changing. This transition is happening in an especially dramatic way within the United States. According to the *New York Times*,

> The Census Bureau projects that by 2042, Americans who identify themselves as Hispanic, black, Asian, American Indian, Native Hawaiian, and Pacific Islander will together outnumber non-Hispanic whites.
>
> In other words, in a little more than a generation, the U.S. will be a "majority minority" country, with ethnic and racial minorities constituting a majority of the nation's population.
>
> "No other country has experienced such rapid racial and ethnic change," says Mark Mather, a demographer with the Population Reference Bureau in Washington, D.C.
>
> The main reason for the accelerating change, according to the Census Bureau, is higher birthrates among immigrants, along with an increase in the number of foreigners coming to the United States.[2]

What does "The Age of Cultural Diversification" mean for you? It means that an understanding of cross-cultural issues and methods is vital. Those who refuse to venture into, explore, and learn about other nations and the ways of life of their citizens will be culturally illiterate in the twenty-first century and will likely experience eventual culture shock.

In this sense, we must be international citizens to be effective in our times. Cultural literacy has a direct bearing on your ability to understand, communicate with, engage in discourse with, and influence cultures different from your own. Living in an age of cultural diversity means giving up a fear of other nations and ethnic groups, becoming informed and knowledgeable about them, and being willing to bridge cultural differences for the sake of effective communication, expressing the love of God to others, and sharing the gospel.

Moreover, the Age of Cultural Diversification means that leadership training in business, education, and the church must prepare people for multicultural experiences. The mandate of the church has always been multinational and multicultural in scope. The twenty-first century church, therefore, requires a multinational, interracial, trans-generational approach that transcends any particular nation's social or political agenda. We must be willing to change old, ineffective methods, modes, and attitudes to meet the needs of today.

> *We must be willing to change ineffective methods, modes, and attitudes to meet the needs of today.*

The Age of Mergers and Networking

In the past, most companies remained independent and were owned by citizens of the countries in which they were located. Today, that is not a guarantee, by any means. Companies are merging with other companies, either by mutual agreement or forced takeovers. Connections between both similar and diverse businesses are creating innovative partnerships. Foreign companies or nations are buying real estate and businesses in other countries. In addition, international trade and the ease of communication are connecting people of like interests and beliefs who live in distinct areas around the world.

What does "The Age of Mergers and Networking" mean for you? For one thing, it assures the continuation of change in your everyday life. A foreign company may buy the business for which you work. Your company may experience a hostile takeover one day and be dismantled the next. How will you respond to this?

On the other hand, an increased ability to network may mean that you make a connection through the Internet with a citizen of another country who shares the same life vision that you do. Through your e-mail correspondence, you form a strong friendship that leads to the establishment of a ministry that cares for the needs of orphans in a war-torn country. Or, the Age of Mergers and Networking may mean that you are able to connect your business with another business that can help you handle an aspect of your company in a more efficient way. Again, we have the choice of trying to hide from the reality of changes or dealing with them forthrightly and with a dedication to deriving benefits from them that will enable us to fulfill our purposes in the world.

The Age of Longevity of Life

With the availability of better nutrition and accessible health services, many people, particularly in Western countries, are living longer and more productive lives. While, for many people, affordable health care is becoming an issue, Western nations still have access to the most up-to-date medical care and medicines in the world. Longevity of life means that many people will be healthy and productive for a greater number of years than the generations before them. Longevity also means that people will need financial resources to see them through their later years, which could extend into their eighties, nineties, and beyond.

What does "The Age of Longevity of Life" mean for you? It means that you will have to make decisions about what you will do with your health and increased years. Will you use them to fulfill your vision and promote God's purposes in the world, or will you waste them on frivolous or selfish pursuits? Will you take advantage of the variety of nutritional foods available, or will you decide to consume junk food and food with chemical additives, increasing your chances of illness and other physical problems? Will you make sound financial plans to save adequate reserves for the future, taking into consideration the uncertainty of Social Security and investments in the stock market? These are challenging but necessary questions to answer in our times.

The Age of Technology

Across the world, technology continues to develop rapidly, especially in such areas as computers, cell phones, and other electronic devices. As fast as one innovation or invention is accepted and absorbed by people, another seems to replace it. If you are young, you probably integrate these innovations very quickly. If you are older, these changes can seem bewildering, and various devices may seem to have no value to you. However, this perspective is not always the case. People in their seventies, eighties, and nineties are signing on to e-mail accounts—often to keep in touch with children and grandchildren. Music lovers of every age are enjoying the technology and convenience of iPods.

What does "The Age of Technology" mean for you? Rapid changes in technology have ramifications in many areas of our lives, including health (ranging from sleep deprivation from constant use of communication devices to anxiety and confusion over adapting to new products), business (positioning your company to be in the forefront of efficient business systems and services), and education (obtaining knowledge and skills for emerging jobs).

Whatever your age or situation, the challenge is to allow technology to *benefit* you—not *control* you. Are you in charge of the technology you use, or is it in charge of you? Do you always need to be online or talking on the phone to someone, or can you put those things aside to attend to other necessary issues? Do you avoid all technology, or are you willing to see its positive contributions? We must discover how to respond efficiently and wisely in an age of technology.

> *Whatever your age or situation, the challenge is to allow technology to benefit you— not control you.*

The Age of Political and Religious Transformation

What issues are affecting the political and religious atmosphere of our world? The *political* transformation taking shape is a transition from the dominance of superpowers to the idea of a community of nations. One of the manifestations of this trend is a movement among some countries to expand the United Nations Security Council to include more than just five permanent nations—China, France, the Russian Federation, the United Kingdom, and the United States—and ten rotating nonpermanent members, which have two-year terms. One hundred ninety-two nations belong to the UN, but all must abide by the decisions of the Security Council. The argument some nations are making is that this arrangement no longer works. They are saying, "We also want a vote; we need to be able to contribute to what happens in the world." Many of the leadership structures in place in our world still reflect the post-World War II era, as well as the Colonial era, and both of these eras are now in the past. What will take their place?

Countries around the world are asking to be respected as equal partners and sovereign nations within the community of nations—regardless of their size or economic strength. They desire equal access, equal opportunity, and equal value. The idea is that leadership should be a shared responsibility with collaboration and cooperation among nations rather than a few nations dictating to the others.

I believe that another significant component of transformation is that God is raising up the formerly opposed, rejected, and ignored peoples of the Third World to places of leadership, influence, and effective ministry in the world. I will return to this concept in greater detail in a later chapter.

What do these political changes mean for you? If these prove to be ongoing trends in the world, will you respond rather than react to them? Both the traditional leaders of the world and the emerging leaders will need to be able to respond under these changed circumstances. These are not easy issues to sort out—but we must first deal with the political world as it *is* rather than the way we *wish* it was. Then, we can build from there.

The *religious* transformations occurring in our world are also momentous. First, global Christianity is undergoing changes that demand urgent assessment and understanding. Again, we have seen the rise of significant and effective national ministers in many Third World countries. These areas were traditionally mission fields for denominations and churches headquartered in industrialized nations. This change demands a new approach to international missions strategies and makes obsolete a number of traditional outreach methods.

For example, some of those from industrialized countries who led missions efforts believed—or gave the impression they believed—that indigenous leaders were incapable of taking spiritual responsibility for their own nations. Suppose you were a parent, and you observed that your children were not maturing but remaining dependent upon you into their young adult years. You might question the effectiveness of your parenting because independence (followed by interdependence) is a sign of maturity. Likewise, indigenous churches in countries that have been reached by Western missions groups are maturing, and their "parents" must accept and adjust to this change. On the other hand, the spiritual leaders in these emerging nations must actively prepare for the responsibility of guiding and discipling their own people.

A second trend is that the largest and fastest growing churches in the world are in Asia and among developing nations. While the largest church in America has close to fifty thousand people, the largest church in the world—in Korea, under the leadership of pastor David Yonggi Cho—has an estimated membership of 830,000.[3] Africa and South America are other areas of tremendous church growth.

A third trend is the emigration of people adhering to Eastern and Middle Eastern religions to Europe and the United States. Will Europeans and Americans react or respond to these new citizens or residents of their countries? The same issue applies to other nations. For example, Islamic countries are saying they don't want Western culture there. However, Saudi Arabia is bringing in large numbers of Filipinos to work in the nation while, at the same time, wanting them to leave their beliefs at home. Yet how realistic is it to bring a people into your country and then tell them not to live according to their convictions? When people are invited to a new place in order to live and work—especially on a temporary basis—they will inevitably bring their culture and beliefs with them. A good response to religious change is to be sure that our own beliefs and values are strong enough to withstand interaction with cultures that are different from ours.

If the gospel is for the whole world, how can we bring the gospel to all nations and peoples if we choose to separate ourselves from other cultures?

A third trend is that the church is undergoing transformation in regard to cultural diversification. The ethnic makeup of many churches is changing. While many churches in the West used to be primarily Caucasian, a growing number are now a mixture of whites, blacks, and Hispanics.

We must discover, therefore, how we can respond to changing religious realities in our world. We *could* try to hide from these realities. Yet if the gospel is for the whole world, how can we bring the gospel to all nations and peoples if we choose to separate ourselves from other cultures? Jesus did a number of remarkable things in relation to the times in which He lived. Once, He led His disciples through Samaria on His way to Galilee. Culturally, the Jews and the Samaritans did not associate with one another. Yet Jesus wanted His disciples to understand that the gospel message is not just a Jewish message but also one that belongs to all peoples of the world. (See John 4:1–42.) Can we take any other attitude than He did toward people of different races and religions in our times?

The Scriptures say that in heaven, there will be people from *"every nation, tribe, people and language"* (Revelation 7:9). Will you react or respond if the cultural makeup in your church becomes multiethnic? Will you change your perspective on the community of faith, asking God to help you overcome your fears and prejudices? Paul was one of the first believers in Jesus to actively pursue preaching the gospel among the Gentiles. Will you affirm, with him, *"The new self…is being renewed in knowledge in the image of its Creator. Here there is no Greek or Jew, circumcised or uncircumcised, barbarian, Scythian, slave or free, but Christ is all, and is in all"* (Colossians 3:10–11)?

The Age of Rapid Transformation

Change today happens exponentially. A popular YouTube video gives the following examples of our rapidly changing world:

+ China will soon become the country with the highest number of English-speaking people.

+ The top ten jobs that will be in demand in 2010 did not exist in 2004.

+ The U.S. Department of Labor estimates that today's learner will have ten to fourteen jobs by age thirty-eight.

+ One in four workers has been with his current employer for less than a year.

+ In 2008, there were 31 billion searches per month on Google. In 2006, the number was 2.7 billion.

+ The first commercial text message was sent in 1992. Today, the total number of text messages equals the entire population of the planet.

+ It took the medium of radio thirty-eight years to reach a market audience of 50 million people. It took television only thirteen years. The Internet, four years. The iPod, three years. Facebook, two years.

+ The number of Internet devices in 1984 was 1000. In 1992, it was one million. In 2008, it was one billion.

+ A week's worth of information in the *New York Times* contains more information than people were likely to encounter in their entire lifetimes in the eighteenth century.

+ Four exabytes of unique information is generated every year, more than in the previous five thousand years.

+ Technology doubles every two years.

+ Half of everything a tech student in a four-year program learns is outdated by his third year of study.

+ A Japanese company has successfully tested a fiber-optic cable that can send 14 trillion bytes of information per second. That is the equivalent of 2660 CDs or 210 million phone calls.[4]

This list is a fitting conclusion to our discussion of the worldwide tides of change we're currently experiencing. How will you respond to the rapid transformation taking place all around you? Here are just two approaches: You may buy new technology that will aid you in furthering your vision. Or, you may find a role teaching others the value of filtering out the "noise" of constant communications so they can focus on God and His plans for their lives. Both of these responses are valid—and necessary. Seek to discover how you can best benefit from momentous change and use it to contribute something positive to others.

Paradigm Shift

The above statistics put our need to respond rather than react to change into even greater perspective, don't they? Sweeping change is exciting to some people. For others, such change threatens their mental and emotional equilibriums. No matter what nation, culture, or outlook we come from, we must know how to respond to the rapid change that is happening around us, to us, through us, and within us. We have to acknowledge the transitional tide of change and deal with it instead of allowing the tide to rise over our heads and drown us.

Sometimes, we try to stand in one spot—figuratively speaking—and say, "This is it. This is as far as I want to go." We don't want to move with the stream of the history of humanity. However, we also need to remember that the story of our world is not ultimately about history but HIS story. It is God's story, and He's always moving us forward in the fulfillment of His purposes.

We can initiate change only by moving into the future.

Those who train themselves to interpret changing times can look downstream and say, "I see a bend coming up; I'm not sure exactly what's around that bend, so I have to be prepared for anything." Yet for many people, the world has already turned a bend, and they're not sure they like what they've discovered there. Certainly, there are both positive and negative changes to address. But we can initiate change only by moving into the future.

A word that has become a common part of our everyday language in recent years is *paradigm*. A paradigm refers to a model, pattern, or way of thinking and acting. When change occurs in a paradigm, it is called a *paradigm shift*. Such a shift occurs during a generational transfer—when old styles become inadequate as a result of new demands and outdated methods cannot be used in resolving new problems. The present providential tide of transitional change requires a paradigm shift on our part. Those who fail to understand the times and seasons and don't discover how to participate in them will find themselves irrelevant in our changing world.

He that will not apply new remedies must expect new evils, for time is the greatest innovator.
—Francis Bacon, philosopher, statesman, and author

PERSONAL PURPOSE AND CHANGE
Let Your Purpose Guide You through Times of Transition

Chosen…according to the plan of him who works out everything
in conformity with the purpose of his will.
—Ephesians 1:11

Throughout this book, I have emphasized that we must persevere in our God-given purposes in the midst of change, and that we must use change to fulfill these purposes. Yet how do we discover God's purposes for our lives so that we can initiate and persist in purposeful change? Let's begin to explore this topic by looking at two major ways of understanding God's purposes.

Change and God's Purposes

God's Promises Are His Purposes for You

God's promises are central to His purposes for your life. When I first came to understand this principle, it helped me to progress and succeed in my purpose. Let's look at this statement again: God's promises are central to *His* purposes for your life—not your own purposes apart from Him. Though God's love for us is incalculable, His promises are not only for us but, more importantly, for the fulfillment of His plans in the world, of which each of us is a significant part.

I like to use this illustration when describing God's intent: When you buy a product from a manufacturer—for example, a camera or a car—a booklet is supplied along with that product. This booklet is often called a *manual*. The manual is the manufacturer's "mind" concerning that product, summarized in one convenient publication. In essence, the creator sends his mind along with his product so that you can understand it—at least to some degree—as he does. Manuals often contain the request, "Before using this product, please read this manual completely." In other words, "Please learn my mind concerning this product completely. Then will you be able to use it as it was intended."

Do you read the manuals that accompany the products you buy—*completely?* Most people don't.

Find a manual in your house from any product and look at the last few pages. Often, you will find one section that says "Warranty" and another that says "Guarantee." Warranty has to do with promise, and guarantee has to do with commitment. The manufacturer is pledging the reliability of both the individual product you have just purchased and the confidence you can place in its name. In many cases, manufacturers really don't care about the customers. They don't even know them. People walk into stores and buy their products, but the manufacturers don't personally know the individuals buying them. Yet when people get the booklets, they're filled with promises: This product will do this, it will do that; it can do this; it can do that. After describing these things, the manufacturer says, "We guarantee it." It also says, in effect, "Now, if you follow these instructions for maintaining it, we'll guarantee that we'll replace the product if it's defective and something happens to go wrong." What are they interested in? The integrity of their own name. They'll pay the cost of shipping the defective product, replace it free of charge, and ship it back to you at their own expense. What are they paying for? They're paying for protecting their name, because they have made a promise. Their promise is this: the product is supposed to provide a certain function. If it is dysfunctional, they will make it right.

We are "products" of our Creator God, and we are given both an internal manual and an external one. God placed the internal one inside us. King Solomon wrote, "[God] *has made everything beautiful in its time. He has also* **set eternity in the hearts of men;** *yet they cannot fathom what God has done from beginning to end*" (Ecclesiastes 3:11, emphasis added). Through this "*eternity*" in our hearts, we have some kind of internal knowledge of the existence of our Creator and of His standards. Our external manual is God's revealed Word—His "mind," which He desires us to know. In addition to being called God's Word, this manual is also known as the Scriptures, or the Bible.

After their creation, human beings abused the product—themselves—ignoring the knowledge of God in their hearts. Yet the external manual includes a warranty and a guarantee. God has made promises to His product in which He assures us, "If something's not working, return it to Me, the Manufacturer, and I will replace the broken parts at no charge." Then, the product will be able to function as it was intended to. Why does He do this? He does so to protect His name. He stands behind what He creates—which was meant for good, not wrong, and for the fulfillment of His purposes for the world. When we offer our broken lives to Him, He restores us through the sacrifice of His Son, Jesus, and we can then learn how we were originally intended to live.

Jesus said,

> *Do not worry, saying, "What shall we eat?" or "What shall we drink?" or "What shall we wear?" For the pagans run after all these things, and your heavenly Father knows that you need them. But seek first his kingdom and his righteousness, and all these things will be given to you as well. Therefore do not worry about tomorrow, for tomorrow will worry about itself. Each day has enough trouble of its own.*
> (Matthew 6:31–34)

When we are aligned with God's purposes, "*all these things*" we need in life come with the warranty. It doesn't matter what changes in our lives; God never changes, and He always fulfills His promises. God's name is stamped on you, and He's going to protect His name.

After Moses led the Israelites out of Egypt through God's power-ful signs and miracles, Moses went separately, accompanied by his aide, Joshua, to meet with God on Mount Sinai and to receive instructions for the Israelites. While Moses and Joshua were away, the rest of the Israelites thought Moses had been gone too long. They imagined he had died or had decided not to come back. So, they made a golden calf and started worship-ping it, saying that it—rather than God, the great I Am—had delivered them out of Egypt. What follows in the account reinforces the fact that God protects His name.

> The LORD said to Moses, "Go down, because your people, whom you brought up out of Egypt, have become corrupt. They have been quick to turn away from what I commanded them and have made them-selves an idol cast in the shape of a calf. They have bowed down to it and sacrificed to it and have said, 'These are your gods, O Israel, who brought you up out of Egypt.' I have seen these people," the LORD said to Moses, "and they are a stiff-necked people. Now leave me alone so that my anger may burn against them and that I may destroy them. Then I will make you into a great nation." But Moses sought the favor of the LORD his God. "O LORD," he said, "why should your anger burn against your people, whom you brought out of Egypt with great power and a mighty hand? Why should the Egyptians say, 'It was with evil intent that he brought them out, to kill them in the mountains and to wipe them off the face of the earth'? Turn from your fierce anger; relent and do not bring disaster on your people. Remember your servants Abraham, Isaac and Israel, to whom you swore by your own self: 'I will make your descendants as numerous as the stars in the sky and I will give your descendants all this land I promised them, and it will be their inheritance forever.'" Then the LORD relented and did not bring on his people the disaster he had threatened.   (Exodus 32:7–14)

God said, in effect, "Moses, these people have rejected Me. I'm going to kill them." The record says that Moses appealed to God on the basis of His name and promise. "Lord, You told the other nations that these people are Your product, and You put Your name on them. If You destroy them, what will the nations say about Your name?" God accepted Moses' appeal. He continued to work with the Israelites, even though they were "stiff-necked."

He did this not so much for their sake but for the sake of His reputation in the world and His plans for the world through the Israelites. His overarching purposes for the earth take precedence over any individual purposes people have.

God's Vision for You Is Your Purpose

The first way we know God's purposes for us, therefore, is through the promises He's given us, which correspond to the fulfillment of His plans for the world. We can count on Him to do what He has said because He is true to His name. The second way we can know God's purposes is by discovering His individual visions, or destinies, for each of us.

Your presence on earth is not a biological accident, regardless of the circumstances that may have surrounded your birth. You are here because of a divine assignment. Your conception is proof that God, in essence, already completed something in eternity that He desires to manifest on earth through you and your life.

I want to reemphasize that you are not an accident. You are not a mistake. You came to this planet because of destiny—God's ultimate intent for you. *Destiny* refers to the ultimate reasons for your creation.

In terms of a product, purpose refers to the original expectation that the manufacturer had for that product. Builders don't begin to construct their products until the structures are already finished in their minds. When you request a permit to build a house, the local officials want to see your plans for it: they want to see the architecture, the plumbing, the electrical system, and so forth. They want to see it "finished" before they give it their stamp of approval. When they are satisfied that your plumbing won't overflow and that your construction won't cause damaging erosion, they say, "Now, you can start." Therefore, when you see a product beginning to be produced, it is proof that the product is already "finished" in someone's mind.

Proverbs 19:21 says, *"Many are the plans in a man's heart, but it is the Lord's purpose* [His end, His destiny, for that person] *that prevails."* This statement shows us that purpose is more powerful than plans. Purpose precedes plans. God says, in effect, "You have many ideas about your life,

The Lord will guide our steps according to His purposes for us. Our responsibility is to learn to tune in to His direction.

but My purpose for your life, My original intent for you, will prevail." So, even if your plans fail, His purpose will succeed. Purpose is His priority. That truth is very reassuring. Every failure we experience is temporary because He said His purpose will prevail.

Let's look at a similar verse: *"In his heart a man plans his course, but the LORD determines his steps"* (Proverbs 16:9). The Lord will guide our steps according to His purposes for us. Our responsibility is to learn to tune in to His direction:

"For I know the plans I have for you," declares the LORD, "plans to prosper you and not to harm you, plans to give you hope and a future. Then you will call upon me and come and pray to me, and I will listen to you. You will seek me and find me when you seek me with all your heart." (Jeremiah 29:11–13)

Let's explore some additional truths in God's Word about His purposes:

"The plans of the LORD stand firm forever, the purposes of his heart through all generations" (Psalm 33:11). *"All generations"* would include all changes and transitional tides in human history.

"May [God] give you the desire of your heart and make all your plans succeed" (Psalm 20:4). When you are in line with His purposes, God will make your plans succeed, even if others try to prevent them.

"To man belong the plans of the heart, but from the LORD comes the reply of the tongue" (Proverbs 16:1). I interpret this to mean that when you realize the plans God has placed in your heart, you may feel they are so big that you aren't able to fulfill them. You don't believe you have the money, the property, the equipment, or other resources to pursue them. Yet God says, in effect, "Don't worry about that; I'll answer for those things. Write down your plan, and I'll take care of how it's going to be paid for."

In my experience, God may not give you the resources first. He will give you a purpose, vision, or dream that only He can fulfill. He takes responsibility for making sure it is paid for, produced, developed, equipped, staffed, and so forth. So, don't worry about making big plans! If God has placed a big vision in your life, and everyone is telling you to cut back, trust God to give the explanation and to supply what is needed.

> *Praise be to the God and Father of our Lord Jesus Christ, who has blessed us in the heavenly realms with every spiritual blessing in Christ. For he chose us in him before the creation of the world to be holy and blameless in his sight. In love he predestined us to be adopted as his sons through Jesus Christ, in accordance with his pleasure and will—to the praise of his glorious grace, which he has freely given us in the One he loves....In him we were also chosen, having been predestined according to the plan of him who works out everything in conformity with the purpose of his will.* (Ephesians 1:3–6, 11)

God hand-picked you before you were born to fulfill something for Him. You were chosen before creation, and you were born when it was time for you to arrive on earth in order to fulfill your purpose. Paul wrote that God *"in love...predestined us."* *Pre* means "before." *Destine* means to "determine," "specify," or "mark off by boundaries." This means that before you and I were born, God chose us specifically to be a part of His plan. He knows exactly how each of us fits into it. God says, "I finished you first, and then I backed up and started you." He *"works out everything in conformity with the purpose of his will."* That's a powerful verse. He works out *"everything"*—all things—to conform to His purpose for your life. He didn't say He would work out just the good things or the right things. He works out everything. This means that if you mess up, experience setbacks, or fail at something—in your marriage, your business, your education, your lifestyle—He will keep your purpose going. He will say, "Come back to Me, and don't dwell on this. You're still going to make it. I'm going to use that situation for good. Together, we're going to make it a testimony to My grace and power." No matter what changes happen between where you are and when you fulfill your destiny, these changes are temporary. God still takes all of that and conforms it. In other words, your mistakes are not more powerful than your purpose.

Joseph had a dream in which *"the sun and moon and eleven stars were bowing down to* [him]" (Genesis 37:9). Even though this dream signified the high position he would someday attain in Egypt, at the time, he was tending flocks. When God shows you your destiny, He may not show you the route by which you will reach it. Why? He has designed the route according to His plan and in order to prepare you for your destiny, and the preparation may not be what you like or expect. Joseph became excited when he realized what his destiny would be. Yet he didn't know that in order to reach it, he would have to endure being sold into slavery by his own brothers, being lied about, and being put into prison. Joseph believed in the dream more than his circumstances, however. And God brought him through all his difficulties and made him the equivalent of a prince. Through this position, he helped preserve the inhabitants of Egypt—and his own family—during a severe famine.

No matter how many bad things seem to happen to you, keep saying to yourself, *This is not what I have seen regarding God's vision for my life.* If what you're experiencing now is not the purpose you have been shown, then it is only temporary, because God will see you through. Even if you're experiencing something good right now, if it is not part of the vision, then it is temporary, also. Nothing can stop your destiny if you stay close to your Creator, because He has already purposed what you were born to do.

King David wrote,

The steps of a good man are ordered by the LORD: *and he delighteth in his way. Though he fall, he shall not be utterly cast down: for the* LORD *upholdeth him with his hand.* (Psalm 37:23–24 KJV)

This Bible version emphasizes, "*The steps of a* **good** *man are ordered by the Lord.*" If you are walking in God's will to the best of your ability, then no matter what changes take place, He has you covered. If you lose your job, that didn't happen without God knowing it. If you are faithful to God and are obeying His Word as best you can, that so-called layoff or firing was actually God laying hold of your course and redirecting it. The Lord will uphold you.

I especially like Psalm 57:2–3, which says, "*I cry out to God Most High, to God, who fulfills his purpose for me. He sends from heaven and saves me, rebuking those who hotly pursue me; God sends his love and his faithfulness.*"

God set your destination before He created you. He gave you a purpose, then He gave you birth, and now He commits Himself to fulfill it for you. If anyone tries to stop you, He'll get *him*. God is going to protect you as you develop whatever you were born to do. Heaven is on the side of God's purpose for your life.

My wife and I once had a chance to visit Egypt. We toured the Sinai Desert, where we saw pyramids and were shown the long route people used to travel from Israel to Egypt. We learned that in the desert, flash floods sometimes occurred. These would happen when it rained in the mountains, and the water ran down from the mountains and through the desert. Water would seemingly show up in the desert from nowhere. Yet the inhabitants of the desert used this change for their benefit by digging big pits to catch this water whenever it came. They would use the cistern for their own drinking water and for watering their camels. So, these pits were all over the desert. At any given time, a pit might be empty or full. This was probably the kind of pit Joseph's brothers threw him into. The important point is that it was the right pit. The cistern was right next to the road that went from Israel to Egypt. It just so happens that a caravan came right alongside the pit on that particular road, giving Joseph's brothers the opportunity to sell him to merchants going to Egypt, making him a slave. Yet this seeming calamity was Joseph's free ride to his princely position.

Why does God position us in various places in life? God positions us to influence others, to change the course of events, and to protect His purposes. This is why one of the most important things you must do is to discover your position in life. What were you born to do?

> *God positions us to influence others, to change the course of events, and to protect His purposes.*

Some of us get put into pits, but they're the right pits if our steps are ordered by the Lord. If Joseph had been in a different pit, those particular traders never would have purchased him, and he wouldn't have gotten to Egypt and become a ruler. As we wait in the pit for God to work, we must remember that there's a caravan on the way. This is how God works through change. Whether you're in the pit or the palace right now, the Lord is ordering your steps as you trust in Him.

Psalm 138:8 says, "*The LORD will fulfill his purpose for me.*" It continues, "*Your love, O LORD, endures forever—do not abandon the works of your hands.*" In other words, God will never abandon or cancel what He gave you birth to do. He is committed to it. That's how strong purpose is. *He* will not abandon your purpose, but the question is, will you abandon it? Are you committed to it? You have to answer this question for yourself. No outside force or circumstance can stop God's destiny for your life. Only you can stop it—by ignoring it, rebelling against it, or giving up on it entirely. God does not want you to miss what He's already guaranteed for you to accomplish.

God makes clear in Isaiah, "*I make known the end from the beginning, from ancient times, what is still to come. I say: My purpose will stand, and I will do all that I please.…What I have said, that will I bring about; what I have planned, that will I do*" (Isaiah 46:10–11). Again, what God is saying is that He always sets the end before the beginning. I remind myself of this truth as an encouragement in the midst of difficulties. If you forget that your end is already finished, you'll become discouraged on your way there. You have to remember what God has said. Tell yourself, *My purpose is finished. I'm on my way there.* Sometimes, there isn't anyone else around to encourage you, and people are quick to send discouragement your way. But God is not worried about your future because, as far as He is concerned, it's already finished. It's in His "past."

Purpose, Time, and Change

In an earlier chapter, we talked about the nature and characteristics of seasons, and how time is the source of change. Recall these principles:

1. Everything that is created—everything that is below the invisible, eternal realm of God—exists in time.

2. Everything that exists in time has a purpose for which there is a season for fulfillment.

3. God's purposes and activities within time are designed for seasons, which in turn require change.

Let's look at some additional principles in regard to time and how they relate to the purposes God has given us.

Time Is One of Our Greatest Gifts on Earth

God made two great lights—the greater light to govern the day and the lesser light to govern the night. He also made the stars. God set them in the expanse of the sky to give light on the earth, to govern the day and the night, and to separate light from darkness. **And God saw that it was good.** (Genesis 1:16–18, emphasis added)

Time is one of the greatest gifts God gave humanity. He affirmed that time is good, and we need to appreciate what we've been given. God placed human beings on earth so that they could enjoy the benefits of time as they learn to know, love, and imitate Him. Eternity has no beginning or end. Time, in my view, is a piece of eternity that God "pulled out" and gave a beginning and end to. Then, He put us in time so that we, too, could experience a beginning and an end to things, grow in maturity and in the character of God, and learn about the creative process and the power of change. I thank God that I live in time right now. In a sense, time gives us the opportunity to prepare for "forever."

Time Allows Us to Live Life in Seasons

Second, time allows us to live life in seasons and to oversee our visions in increments. Isn't it nice that you don't have to live your life all at once? God allows us to spread out our lives in days, months, and years. At any given moment, we have a past, a present, and a future. We should thank Him for this privilege.

Time provides us the opportunity to put our priorities in order and to establish change in our lives. You can decide to do something this year differently than the way in which you did it last year. Time allows you to make that kind of choice. So, time is a benefit in the sense that we can say, "I used to do that in years past, but I don't do it anymore." Likewise, whatever you were *not* doing last year to initiate change to fulfill your purpose, you can make a decision to do *now*. You can change your behavior in order to have a different experience. I appreciate these dimensions. In the past, I used

Time provides us the opportunity to put our priorities in order and to establish change in our lives.

to be a certain way. In the present, I am another way. In the future, I plan to be a different way. That's what time allows. Many of us are happy about this reality, because we are glad to be past our pasts.

Of course, our time on earth is limited, and the reality of time shouldn't cause us to be complacent and lazy, thinking, *I can always do that* (seek a closer relationship with God, pursue my purpose, develop maturity) *in the future.* We never know when our time on earth will be completed. Yet, in the meantime, we are allowed the time to make steady progress toward growing in God's character and fulfilling our visions.

Time Is Our Indicator That Nothing on Earth Lasts Forever

Third, time is our guarantee that nothing on earth will last forever. God has given us time so that we can have a beginning and an end. You are going through certain things right now that time will deal with. Your pain, your frustration, and your disappointments will come to an end. We hear people say such things as, "I was injured last year, but I'm healed now," "I got a divorce two years ago, but I feel I can move on now," "I was abused twenty years ago, but I have peace of mind now." Time allows us to be removed from the past. If you had a past that was not good, for whatever reason, you can now live a new life.

> If anyone is in Christ, he is a new creation; the old has gone, the new has come! All this is from God, who reconciled us to himself through Christ and gave us the ministry of reconciliation.
> (2 Corinthians 5:17–18)

> Praise be to the God and Father of our Lord Jesus Christ, the Father of compassion and the God of all comfort, who comforts us in all our troubles, so that we can comfort those in any trouble with the comfort we ourselves have received from God.   (2 Corinthians 1:3–4)

Time Was Given for Purpose to Be Fulfilled

Let's return to Ecclesiastes 3:1, which says, "*There is a time for everything, and a season for every activity under heaven.*" We see here that time was created for a purpose. Next, let's look at Ecclesiastes 3:10: "*I have seen the burden God has laid on men.*" What is this "*burden*"?

*He has made everything beautiful in its time. He has also set eternity
in the hearts of men; yet they cannot fathom what God has done from
beginning to end.*   (Ecclesiastes 3:11)

The burden God has placed on all human beings—at least, one aspect
of it—is that He has designed everything to occur within a certain time.
This means that we have to find out as soon as possible what we're meant
to do in life, because it's been given a certain period in which to be accomplished. We need to fulfill our purposes on earth before we die. Therefore,
the "burden," or pressure, is on us to find out our assignments so that we
can do them within the time we're supposed to complete them.

Yet another part of this verse says, *"He has also set eternity in the hearts
of men."* Along with a general awareness of Him and of what is right and
wrong, God has placed within every human being His intended purpose
for that person. Remember Isaiah 46:10, *"I make known the end from the beginning"*? God has put your "beginning" and your "end" inside you. You are
a walking destiny. We must keep in mind, as we fulfill our purposes, this
insightful saying of Ralph Waldo Emerson, the poet and essayist: "What
lies before us and what lies behind us are small matters compared to what
lies within us. And when we bring what is within us out into the world,
miracles happen." What is inside us will create the future.

We can summarize these ideas in the following principles:

1. Time was given for purpose to be fulfilled.

2. You don't have forever to fulfill your purpose. There's a season for
    everything.

3. Your purpose is God's established "end," which you are to begin and
    complete.

Seasons Have Their Own Inherent Blessings

In the Bahamas, mangoes are a common and popular fruit. Have you
ever tried to pick a piece of fruit when it wasn't yet ripe? You can pick a
mango when it's green—it will be very small and hard. You can do it: the
tree won't fight you. The problem is, you will not be able to enjoy the experience if you try to eat it.

Similarly, you can take things in life out of season, and no matter what you do, they will never work for you. Seasons bring their own inherent blessings. If you know that everything in your life has a season, and if you continue to study and discern your seasons as you seek God's direction, everything will work in your favor. When it's your season, even your enemies may become your friends—or, if not, they won't be able to stop you. When it's your season, doors that had been closed will start to open. When it's your season, people who didn't like you will start helping you, and they won't be able to explain why. When it's your season, things that had been difficult will become easy. The things you've been fighting to accomplish will fight to *come* to you. This is why I am open to whatever is seasonal in my life.

> *God's words will be like buckets that go deep down inside you and pull up ideas and dreams you never knew you had.*

Proverbs 20:5 says, *"The purposes of a man's heart are deep waters, but a man of understanding draws them out."* I desire to be a *"man of understanding"* in your life through this book, helping to draw out your God-given purposes so that you can see them and act on them in season. The purposes inside us are deep. As you read and understand God's Word, His words will be like buckets that go deep down inside you—where He has set eternity in your heart—and pull up ideas and dreams you never knew you had. Psalm 37:4 says, *"Delight yourself in the LORD and he will give you the desires of your heart."* God will enable you to fulfill the desires He has planned for you since before time began—desires He has placed in your heart.

Your destiny has already been established and finished in eternity, but you were born to begin it. You are at the beginning of your "end" right now. You are in progress toward that end, and you have to stay on course. Keep moving steadily toward your purpose, no matter what. Let your purpose take you through the pressures, challenges, and changes of life.

I must be about My Father's business.
—Jesus Christ (Luke 2:49 NKJV)

THE GREATEST HINDRANCE TO POSITIVE CHANGE
Outdated Methods and Traditions Stifle Innovation

In times of change, learners inherit the Earth, while the learned find themselves
beautifully equipped to deal with a world that no longer exists.
—Eric Hoffer, writer, philosopher,
and Presidential Medal of Freedom recipient

While change is the greatest motivator of innovation, *tradition* (including a reliance on past experiences) is the greatest hindrance to the positive changes you desire—for your life, community, nation, and world. By *tradition*, I am not referring to timeless truths. Good judgment and sound principles never change. Many of the points I'm discussing in this book apply to all times because they are based on the truth of God's Word and proven principles. But doing something because "it's always been done that way," or engaging in practices that have no real solid foundation, is a form of perpetuating tradition when innovation is called for.

To illustrate, let's consider some of the factors surrounding the financial crisis that hit consumers in 2008. Reckless monetary practices had become the norm for some financial institutions, and certain banks kept issuing risky loans. Their irresponsibility caught up with them. Not only did record numbers of homeowners default on their loans, but many companies also suffered irreversible losses. Many people were laid off from their jobs because of direct and indirect consequences of these practices. What many people thought was standard operating procedure was a disaster in the making.

In contrast, other financial institutions—both large and small—did not engage in these or other risky practices. They continued to follow proven principles and monetary policies, and they were unshaken by the financial crisis. They continued to have plenty of money to loan, and they didn't have to worry about laying off employees or shutting their doors.

There are sound business practices that should be passed along to future generations, and there are antiquated or foolish practices that should not perpetuated. In considering change versus tradition, therefore, we must be discerning and allow wisdom to guide us.

The Pull of Tradition

> There are practices that transcend change and generations. Yet traditional ways can hinder us from thinking creatively in addressing the needs of today.

With that as background, I want to discuss the lure of tradition, which will keep you from making progress in life. When we have used a method that has been effective and successful, we will be tempted to keep using it, whether it's a program, a system, a project, a style, or a modus operandi. Again, there are practices and methods that transcend change and generations. Yet traditional ways of thinking or of doing things can hinder us from thinking creatively in addressing the needs of today. Earlier, I gave the example of those who still hold out hope of regaining their former jobs when the industries they used to work in are now obsolete. Their traditional mind-sets concerning these industries—remembering them in their heyday rather than in their current reality—prevents them from thinking of new vocational opportunities and traps them in anger and regret.

In this context, tradition is taking something that was once successful and attempting to pass it on to the next generation. We think that since something has worked for us, then it should and must *always* work. Interestingly, the English words *treason* and *tradition* have the same word origin, because both refer to "handing over" something. Let us consider this: When we try to hand over tradition rather than truth, are we betraying the next generation? Are we limiting their ability to respond to new challenges and changes? Are we limiting our own abilities to meet the needs of today?

Tradition and the Fear of Change

The fear of change is often motivated by a misguided clinging to tradition. Tradition is good until it becomes useless. Tradition is valuable as long as it makes room for the future. But when tradition threatens the emergence of the future, it must be buried. As it marches toward progress, change demands the surrender of obsolete human traditions.

Discard Your "Jawbones"

One of the best-known characters in the Bible is Samson. Among his greatest feats of strength was his destruction of one thousand Philistines using only the jawbone of a donkey as a weapon. Samson used this instrument to protect the Israelites from their enemies.

> As [Samson] *approached Lehi, the Philistines came toward him shouting. The Spirit of the* LORD *came upon him in power. The ropes on his arms became like charred flax, and the bindings dropped from his hands. Finding a fresh jawbone of a donkey, he grabbed it and struck down a thousand men. Then Samson said, "With a donkey's jawbone I have made donkeys of them. With a donkey's jawbone I have killed a thousand men."* (Judges 15:14–16)

If Samson had lived today, he might have hired a marketing manager, who would have helped him to patent that jawbone, manufacture it in quantity, and sell it to the highest bidder as a proven weapon—whether or not it would work for that person as it had for him.

Yet Samson apparently didn't think in those terms. The account of the incident concludes, *"When he finished speaking, he threw away the jawbone"* (verse 17). He saw no need to enshrine the jawbone, even though he had won a great victory with it. He realized that it wasn't the jawbone but the power of God that had enabled him to succeed.

Are you hoarding your "jawbones" of the past, or are you willing to throw away even what worked previously because you recognize that change demands that a new method be used? Tradition can be defined as success that is frozen in time but that you try to bring into the future, even as change is making the old ways irrelevant.

Corrective Invention

As we have discussed, some people react to change by doing nothing. Yet when change is forcing a transformation in your life or in society, then maintaining the status quo will not suffice. When we face unexpected or even anticipated problems in society, change is essentially saying to us, "Invent something to correct me." Let's return to the example of the financial crisis that hit in 2008. With the interconnectedness of national and international banks and other financial institutions, and the danger of collapse for some of these institutions, the United States government entered the picture to guarantee the solvency of companies or to essentially buy them out. Some people supported this action, while others feared that the United States was becoming a Socialist nation. The idea of nationalizing major assets in the economy was described by the government as an emergency response to prevent more calamity. Either this practice will continue, or change will challenge people to think of a different solution. Again, change drives you to consider, create, invent, and construct unexplored potential you never knew you had. As I've said before, I have great faith in the human spirit because that spirit is made in God's image, and it is His nature to be creative. We will find a way because we will be inventive.

Ways We Hold On to Tradition

Relying on tradition, when we should be integrating ourselves in change, can take various forms. Let's look at some of the major expressions of this approach.

Resting on Earlier Successes

I mentioned briefly in a previous chapter when listing "The Benefits of Change" that we can become overly satisfied by our past successes. We can become so mesmerized by the history we have created that we stop making history. Sadly, our complacency often undermines our potential for present and future progress. We celebrate our accomplishments at the expense of new achievements.

However, while we have a tendency to focus on what we have already accomplished, change has a way of detaching us from our earlier achievements. It keeps us from becoming enamored of our own past "greatness." Because most of us won't leave past successes behind easily, change keeps us from getting stuck in a level of success and achievement that negates or suppresses our true potential.

> *Change keeps us from getting stuck in a level of success and achievement that negates or suppresses our true potential.*

Success can become a prison when we convert it, as we often do, into a monument. It can also become a house in which the creative spirit of humanity decides to settle down. Eventually, it can become the permanent address of unreleased or unfulfilled potential. History has proven that the only way to dislodge the human spirit trapped in that house is for some form of drastic change to destroy the house—the figurative equivalent of a hurricane, tornado, or fire. Out of the ruins of that house emerges a human spirit that is reactivated to be creative, to be progressive, to think in new ways, to invent new responses to life, and to develop new solutions to the new problems that were created by the change. We've heard the saying, "Necessity is the mother of invention." That statement is certainly true in this context. In other words, the human spirit does not normally seem to progress unless it is under pressure, and that pressure is usually initiated or introduced by change.

Being Preoccupied with Past Methods

The average person doesn't lead change—he is led by change. This is often because he is preoccupied with tradition—with past ways of doing things. We don't have to be *consciously* preoccupied with tradition to have this mind-set. We can simply take certain established methods and practices for granted and therefore be blinded to other ways of thinking and to new possibilities.

I'm continually amazed at inventors, artists, and businesspeople who are always moving from one thing to the next and achieving great things. Bill Gates, cofounder of Microsoft, has this quality. He never seems to stop innovating or forging new paths. This is why he leads change, and change doesn't lead him.

After earning my bachelor's and master's degrees in the United States, I returned to the Bahamas in 1980 with a vision for creating Bahamas Faith Ministries International (BFMI) and developing Third World leaders. As I moved forward with my plans, I encountered resistance and misunderstanding, because I was attempting something unheard of at the time. What I was doing was not traditional for a Bahamian. I was leading change by creating a new "product" in an environment that wasn't used to it.

The forces of change that I initiated resulted in the creation of an organization headquartered on a small island that now reaches nations around the globe. The tides of change transformed my life, as well as the lives of hundreds of thousands who have been educated and inspired through the organization's conferences and through my radio, television, and Internet programs, books, and international speaking engagements.

If I had been preoccupied with the past, I never would have started BFMI or my work with Third World leaders. In fact, I probably never would have sought to go to college or to realize my God-given vision. Those who are caught up in the past and who merely accept the status quo will be led by change, not the other way around. Yet anyone who leads change will contribute significantly to his or her generation.

One way that we define greatness is by the amount of positive change a person has created. What would the world be like without the influences of the patriarchs Abraham and Moses, of the monarchs David and Solomon, or of the early church leaders who *"turned the world upside down"* (Acts 17:6 KJV)? What would America have become without the influences of George Washington and Abraham Lincoln? What would the second half of the twentieth century have been like without Martin Luther King Jr.,

Mother Teresa, Nelson Mandela, and Ronald Reagan? These were people who were, in a sense, revolutionaries. They forged new frontiers.

And, of course, the One who has influenced the world the most is Jesus Christ. The amount of positive change He has initiated can never be calculated.

People who can forge new frontiers—whether on a large or small scale—will be successful through change. The key to future *failure*, therefore, is to be preoccupied with the past and to cling to traditional ways of doing things.

Relying on Experience as Our Best Teacher

When experience is your *best* or *only* teacher, your progress in life will be thwarted. We've been taught by our parents and our culture that experience is our most valuable instructor. Experience is a very good teacher, especially when we learn from our mistakes. Yet my study of history had led me to believe that those who lead change often have to "overlook" experience in favor of attempting the untried. Those who rely only on experience can undermine their futures. If you cling to an experience that cannot accommodate change, this can cause you to become a victim of that change. He who worships the past will remain there.

When You're Through Changing, You're Through

The greatest human temptation is to believe that you have arrived. We are all prone to move toward security, but security itself is an illusion. For example, consider the term *Social Security*. *Social* refers to society; *security* refers to permanence. Yet this idea is impossible: society can never be permanent. Nothing in this life can be secured. For some years, the Social Security program in the United States has been uncertain. Even before the 2008 financial crisis, the program was said to be in jeopardy. First, the government has borrowed Social Security funds for other purposes. Second, with a large older population and a much smaller younger population, the funds won't be there when the younger generations reach retirement age. Now, the fate of Social Security is even less certain. The government can really no longer guarantee that people will receive any money as retirement security, even though people have paid into the program all their working lives. Private sector programs, such as investments in mutual funds, are also unreliable. There's always a risk that these funds will lose money, a reality all too many investors in IRAs and 401ks experienced in 2008 and 2009.

> *Most people think there's a place at which they can arrive where they can stop changing. If this were possible, they would also stop growing and developing.*

Yet because most people gravitate to the idea of security, they think that there's a place or a condition at which they can arrive in life where they can stop changing. They may not realize that, if this were possible, they would also stop growing, expanding, progressing, moving, and developing. This place or condition of security is often called "retirement." They believe that when they arrive there after working hard for most of their lives, they will be secure. Actually, if you've reached a place where you no longer change, you have just entered the "cemetery" of humanity. It's a living cemetery, but when you are through changing, you're "through."

No one can "retire" from change. Yet retirement is defined by many people as a time when they don't have to think about change but can pursue leisure, instead. For example, someone about to retire may think, in effect, *I'm not going to work, I'm not going to think actively, and I'm not going to create anything. I'm just going to play golf. I'm going to have the same friends from the same retirement club and meet on the same golf course every day for the rest of my life.* Given this scenario, my conclusion is that this person is basically finished as a human being. We just need to sing the final hymn at his funeral.

The desire to keep growing as a person, and the willingness to keep responding to change, are evidence that someone is still living among us. His ability to keep changing until he leaves the earth is our only indication that he is still alive. "When you are through changing, you're 'through'" is just as true for companies, countries, communities, and families as it is for individuals. If a company believes that it has *the* formula for success, which never needs to vary, the company has just sealed its own demise. If a community thinks it has reached a perfect state of governance or growth, it has just begun to decline. If you think you have your life wrapped up, you have just "died."

I suggest that the older you grow, the more change you should initiate because change will keep you alive. It will enable you to be a contributing member of the human family. You can't wait for things to happen anymore. You have to *make* them happen. To do this, you have to work against the traditional perspective of our culture, which promotes the opposite. The older people grow, the less change they're encouraged to be involved in. People begin looking for security, stability—in essence, "tradition."

Yet eighty- and ninety-year-olds who are always active and traveling, visiting new places, are those who usually have sound minds and physical energy. Moreover, those who can't be physically active but have energetic spirits are always inspiring to be around. They're continually talking of experiences that animate them. They are the life of the party, no matter how old they are, because somehow they have learned the secret that change is to life what oxygen is to the body. It keeps giving you new, internal energy.

The goal in life is not to enshrine the history of our lives but to create additional history. The history that we read about in books and see in documentaries and dramas may be defined as "recorded change." We don't often record normal, everyday things. Instead, history is a record of people and events that have changed human life in some way. Therefore, if you want to leave a mark on history, and not become lost in the machinery of tradition, you *must* initiate or maximize change.

Again, history is really about documented change or documented change *agents*. Historically, we remember those who—in both positive and negative ways—transformed our world. For example, think about all the great warriors in history. Why do people still write and talk about Alexander the Great? Because he conquered the known world during his time. Why do people still write and talk about Napoleon? Because he made France into an empire and nearly defeated Russia.

The same principle holds true in modern times. Regardless of your opinion of President Barack Obama, he made history because he brought change. *Change* was the byword of his presidential campaign.

I want to challenge you to step outside the limitations of tradition. Be willing to pay the price for creating something new or improving on something to the point that it functions effectively in a new way. That's what life is about. It's not about maintaining the status quo, but it's about creating a new status.

Initiating change guarantees you a place in history. My prayer is that the change you initiate will be for the improvement of humanity, not its destruction. We remember Adolf Hitler for the destructive change he brought. We remember Nelson Mandela because he was willing to pay the price of twenty-five years in prison for the improvement of his people and for the advancement of human dignity in the world. We remember Jesus for the everlasting, redemptive change that He brought through His life, death, and resurrection.

"Forgetting What Is Behind"

People who initiate change must, in some sense, have short memories. They must not be married to the past or to tradition to the extent that they drag it around with them. Change agents, therefore, need to learn to forget "the way things have always been done."

Paul wrote,

> *I press on, that I may lay hold of that for which Christ Jesus has also laid hold of me. Brethren, I do not count myself to have apprehended; but one thing I do, forgetting those things which are behind and reaching forward to those things which are ahead, I press toward the goal for the prize of the upward call of God in Christ Jesus.*
> (Philippians 3:12–14 NKJV)

We need to be proactive, progressive, and pro-responsive. In this way, we will become the designers of change and not the victims of it.

We need to be people who are not afraid to explore the unknown and who plan for change instead of panicking when it comes.

For you to become an effective responder to change, you must be willing to forget the effects of the previous change and reach for what is ahead. Notice that Paul didn't say we were to *maintain what currently is* but to *reach forward to what is ahead.* We need to be proactive, progressive, and pro-responsive. In this way, we will become the designers of change and not the victims of it.

The Benefit of Inexperience

The cry for change often begins in the hearts of the inexperienced because their aspiration for the unknown generates a spirit of change. For example, lack of experience was identified during the 2008 presidential elections in the United States as the greatest weakness of then presidential candidate Barack Obama. A number of other candidates used experience as their primary qualification to lead. Yet perhaps Obama's inexperience turned out to be his greatest strength among voters because it allowed him to envision and talk about change—and the idea of change resonated with many people. In a parallel way, his challenger, Senator John McCain, promoted his own nontraditional approach to his party and to issues, in addition to his experience, in order to connect with voters.

I'm not saying that experience isn't sometimes helpful or important in initiating change. Think, for example, of inventor Thomas Edison, who kept on experimenting based on both his past failures and his ingeniously creative mind to ultimately invent the electric light bulb, among many other groundbreaking devices. However, experience can sometimes undermine your dreams because you may begin to think of what cannot be done, and why. A lack of experience can allow a person to believe in possibilities without the hindering knowledge of what was possible in the past. In essence, he or she has no reference for restriction.

Perhaps this is why, throughout history, change has always been the rite of passage for youth. Often, when the Creator implemented change, He sought the inexperienced in the affairs of tradition. For example, although King Saul had once seen God do miraculous things, his human experience and shortcomings limited his confidence that he and the rest of the Israelites could defeat the giant Goliath. In contrast, the young David was fearless. He had no precedent of personally warring against the Philistines, and he didn't entertain any thoughts that it was impossible to defeat this giant. He was convinced of God's power and desire to honor His name.

David's innovation was to use a new weapon on the battlefield—a weapon formerly used mainly to protect sheep. He had used his slingshot and deadly aim to help him kill lions and bears that had tried to attack his flock. Therefore, he saw no reason why he couldn't also use it against

Goliath. Tradition said he should wear armor in going against the tough Philistine, and Saul tried to give him his own armor. But David said to Saul, in effect, "I cannot fight in your armor. I must use what I know." (See 1 Samuel 17:21–54.) Innovators will always employ tools that are untested on the field of tradition. They are willing to try the untested to achieve the unknown.

No one approaches life without some experience and tradition behind him—unless that person is an infant! Rather, change agents blend experience and possibility into a *new* experience. Change, therefore, may simply be the introduction of an experience that is different from your old one. Your capacity to learn how to effectively employ new ways of thinking, to use new tools, and to use old tools in a new way will determine whether you will be an initiator of change or a victim of change.

You can judge your age by the amount of pain you feel when you come in contact with a new idea.
—Pearl S. Buck, writer, winner of the Pulitzer prize and Nobel Prize

THE CHALLENGE OF CHANGE
Change Tests and Reveals Who We Are

The most important thing to remember is this: To be ready at any moment to give up what you are for what you might become.
—W. E. B. Du Bois, civil rights activist and cofounder of the NAACP

Change challenges us in many ways, but these can all be distilled into one main challenge: a test of maturity. This is what I was referring to earlier when I talked about the difference between *reacting to* and *responding to* change in life.

Paul wrote, *"And we know that in all things God works for the good of those who love him, who have been called according to his purpose....What, then, shall we say in response to this? If God is for us, who can be against us?"* (Romans 8:28, 31, emphasis added). We have to actively seek what it means to respond to unsettling change rather than react to it. Note that even though God is for us and is working on our behalf, this isn't a guarantee that things in life won't change. When Paul said, *"If God is for us,"* he was about to refer to all the difficulties that can happen to us—and also how we can be conquerors over them. He lists trouble, hardship, persecution, famine, nakedness, danger, and sword (death). (See verse 35.) Again, many people today are teaching that if God is with you, you won't have to go through any difficult experiences. This is weak theology; it causes people to be totally unprepared for times of trouble and change.

Paul indicated that since God was with him, he could have all these experiences and still be mature in his response to them. What was the basis for his confidence? *"If God is for us, who can be against us? He who did not spare his own Son, but gave him up for us all—how will he not also, along with him, graciously give us all things?"* (Romans 8:31–32). God didn't withhold the sacrificial death of His own Son on our behalf. Therefore, we can know that He will also give us everything else we need for this life. As a result, *"in all these things we are more than conquerors through him who loved us"* (verse 37).

Shortly before He was arrested and crucified, Jesus spoke to His disciples about the impending time of pressure and trial they would face. Jesus told them that they would grieve over His death, but that their grief would be turned to joy over His resurrection. Then, He said, *"I have told you these things, so that in me you may have peace. In this world you will have trouble. But take heart! I have overcome the world"* (John 16:33). He had overcome the world, so they didn't need to be afraid, even in the midst of this critical change.

Remember Jesus' parable about the house built on the rock and the house built on the sand? The storm hit both houses equally. Change happens to everyone—to those who are prepared for it and to those who are unprepared for it; to those who acknowledge God and to those who do not acknowledge Him.

> *Everyone who hears these words of mine and puts them into practice is like a wise man who built his house on the rock. The rain came down, the streams rose, and the winds blew and beat against that house; yet it did not fall, because it had its foundation on the rock. But everyone who hears these words of mine and does not put them into practice is like a foolish man who built his house on sand. The rain came down, the streams rose, and the winds blew and beat against that house, and it fell with a great crash.* (Matthew 7:24–27)

Both houses were confronted with the same rain, the same swirling water, and the same wind. Your decision to build your life on the rock rather than the sand does not make you immune from the storm—but it *does* affect the outcome; it does affect how you survive it. Your faith does not always repel change. Rather, change *proves* the reality of your faith.

> *Your faith does not always repel change. Rather, change proves the reality of your faith.*

This is why I say the maturity of your belief system will be tested by change. We can, therefore, list these principles of change and maturity:

1. Change comes to test who we are and who we claim to be.

2. A person's maturity is measured by his or her response to change.

3. Change will always manifest our maturity if it's truly there.

4. Change is a means by which we can *learn* the mature response to unsettling times.

Change Tests Who We Are

I think the apostle Paul was one of the greatest examples and teachers of how to measure maturity in human experience. For example, he wrote to the Philippians:

> *I have learned to be content whatever the circumstances. I know what it is to be in need, and I know what it is to have plenty. I have learned the secret of being content in any and every situation, whether well fed or hungry, whether living in plenty or in want. I can do everything through him who gives me strength.* (Philippians 4:11–13)

In essence, all circumstances were the same to Paul. He didn't let good times or difficult times prevent him from pursuing his purpose in life. *"Who shall separate us from the love of Christ? Shall trouble or hardship or persecution or famine or nakedness or danger or sword?"* (Romans 8:35). This list of difficulties incorporates anything we might experience in life—and worse!—and they imply all the emotions that can accompany them, such as fear, terror, anger, shame, and sorrow. Let's consider how these areas might translate into troubles we experience as we live and work in our various nations. You can add your own applications.

- *Trouble*: temporary illnesses; accidents; misunderstandings between people; a child's learning difficulties; pressures on families, such as infidelity, unplanned pregnancies, or conflicts between parents and children; living amid the influence of gangs.

- *Hardship*: damage or loss to your property; having to work more than one job to make ends meet; taking responsibility for the long-term care of a loved one; not having access to clean water; having to travel miles for medical help.

- *Persecution*: being excluded by others; being falsely accused of something; being gossiped about; being ostracized or somehow penalized for your beliefs; not being allowed to vote; being pressured to support something you don't believe in.

- *Famine and nakedness*: being laid off and having no immediate means of earning money; lacking love from family members; physical droughts that affect the crops you intended to sell or to purchase; not being able to gain the education you desire.

- *Danger*: living in a crime-ridden neighborhood, with frequent occurrences of assaults, rapes, or home invasions; being overcome by a natural disaster, such as a hurricane or a flood; living with the threat of terrorism or other violent acts; having a job that involves the risk of bodily harm.

- *Sword*: experiencing the death of a loved one, a friend, or a community member, whether through natural or unnatural means—such as in the line of duty, car accidents, murder, or genocide.

That is some list. Many more examples could be added. Yet Paul said he was more than a conqueror through all these types of things, because he had confidence that *"in all things God works for the good of those who love him, who have been called according to his purpose"* (Romans 8:28). That's maturity.

Maturity Is Measured by Our Response to Change

Your level of maturity is measured by how you well handle change. In the chapter on "The Greatest Hindrance to Positive Change," we discussed not centering our lives on either past accomplishments or past failures. We looked at Paul's statement, *"One thing I do: Forgetting what is behind and straining toward what is ahead, I press on toward the goal to win the prize for which God has called me heavenward in Christ Jesus*" (Philippians 3:13–14). Paul was saying, in effect, "If you can forget what you did before, and press toward something you haven't done yet, that's maturity."

Based on the above list of trials in life, we can add tragedies and hardships to the things we should not dwell on. Who is able to do this in the midst of life's changes and difficulties? Our answer comes in Paul's next statement: "*All of us who are mature should take such a view of things. And if on some point you think differently, that too God will make clear to you*" (verse 15).

Paul said only mature people can stop living in the past and accept the approaching future. Consider carefully how I am using the word *maturity* here. It refers to responding constructively, no matter what we face in life, instead of merely reacting and thereby causing ourselves further disappointment, pain, and lost potential. Paul was certainly not saying—and neither am I—that it is immature to feel sorrow or to grieve. At one place, he wrote to the Philippians about his friend and fellow worker Epaphroditus, who had fallen sick, "*Indeed he was ill, and almost died. But God had mercy on him, and not on him only but also on me, to spare me sorrow upon sorrow*" (Philippians 2:27). Paul knew sorrow. He also knew deep distress:

> *Maturity refers to responding constructively, instead of merely reacting and thereby causing ourselves further disappointment, pain, and lost potential.*

> We are hard pressed on every side, but not crushed; perplexed, but not in despair; persecuted, but not abandoned; struck down, but not destroyed. We always carry around in our body the death of Jesus, so that the life of Jesus may also be revealed in our body.
>
> (2 Corinthians 4:8–10)

Maturity, therefore, is measured by your capacity to *let go* or to "*forget*" the past and to *build* and *create* the future. Some people mourn for years over what happened, what didn't happen, what could have happened, what they used to do, and how things used to be. Maturity is measured by one's capacity to respond effectively to the unexpected. Those who are mature look to the future and focus on fulfilling their purposes for living.

I travel all over the world, and I encounter all kinds of cultures. Sometimes, I enter a country, and I think, *How do they live under these conditions?* We see others' difficult lifestyles and feel sorry for them, but they're happy because the human spirit finds a way to respond to change and to make it work for them. For example, when gasoline prices were very high, people complained, but they still found a way to buy gas for their cars. Or, they made alternative arrangements, such as carpooling with neighbors, taking the bus or subway, forgoing long road trips, and driving only when they really needed to. Consequently, people forced a change in the situation because, when the demand for gas when down, the price also went down again dramatically.

Life can devastate us when we think that what we are experiencing is a permanent condition. Yet remember that everything is seasonal. If you're down and out right now, look up and smile. Why? It's only a *season*. The Bible says there's a time to weep and a time to laugh. (See Ecclesiastes 3:4.) Circumstances change.

Change Will Manifest the Maturity within You

Change is the greatest revealer of your inner, true maturity. Maturity has nothing to do with age. It has to do with your ability to maintain your balance, perspective, and internal peace in the middle of unexpected chaos. If change debilitates you, immobilizes you, or disarms your mental faculties to the point where they cannot respond and function in a positive and progressive manner, you can be described as immature.

While children are often thought of as immature, we can note some important qualities they possess that will enable us to handle change better. A young child doesn't have the sophisticated perception necessary to properly understand and interpret his environment, which may be swarming with changes. Therefore, he may appear to exhibit qualities of the highest level of maturity, which seeks the benefit or beauty in every situation.

For example, a child sees a truck coming down the street toward him. What is his response? He stands transfixed, fascinated by its powerful-looking size or shiny grille. Or, he sees a fire burning. The flames just appear beautiful to him, and he wants to engage with that fire. He does not yet have the life experience to know the potential dangers in these things or to have developed a healthy fear of being hurt through improper interaction with them. If we observe a child reacting with naïve curiosity rather than necessary caution, we remove him from harm's way, thinking, *He just doesn't understand because he's immature.*

Yet Jesus made this remarkable statement, which contains an important truth we can apply to addressing change: *"Anyone who will not receive the kingdom of God like a little child will never enter it"* (Mark 10:15). Of course, He didn't mean that we should walk in front of a Mack truck or put our hands into fire. I think He was suggesting that we should look at life with the fresh perspective and acceptance of a child. When change occurs, everyone else around you may believe it's chaos; they may think it's danger and destruction. Yet you can approach it as a child would by realizing, *God promises that all things will work together for good, so there's something good I have to look for in this.*

Some people might call that approach unrealistic, but in God's view, it's mature, if it's based on trust in Him. Jesus responded in this way during a violent storm. He and His disciples were crossing a lake by boat when the storm hit. The disciples were beside themselves and feared they would all drown. They looked for Jesus and found Him sleeping on a pillow at the back of the boat! Was this a childish way to react to the circumstances? It seems so. Some children have slept through tornados and never noticed. But did Jesus know something that the disciples didn't know? Absolutely, yes. He knew He could trust in God in the midst of any circumstance.

> *That day when evening came, [Jesus] said to his disciples, "Let us go over to the other side." Leaving the crowd behind, they took him along, just as he was, in the boat. There were also other boats with him. A furious squall came up, and the waves broke over the boat, so that it was nearly swamped. Jesus was in the stern, sleeping on a cushion. The disciples woke him and said to him, "Teacher, don't you care if we drown?" He got up, rebuked the wind and said to the waves, "Quiet! Be still!" Then the wind died down and it was completely calm. He said to his disciples, "Why are you so afraid? Do you still have no faith?" They were terrified and asked each other, "Who is this? Even the wind and the waves obey him!"* (Mark 4:35–41)

The disciples asked Jesus, *"Don't you care if we drown?"*

His reply to them was another question: *"Do you still have no faith?"*

> *Maturity isn't ignoring danger but rather interpreting it correctly so that it becomes a benefit to you rather than a burden.*

Jesus and the disciples both experienced the same situation, much like Jesus' parable of the two houses battered by the storm. Yet the disciples were alarmed; He was calm. They panicked; His faith remained steadfast. Maturity isn't ignoring danger but rather interpreting it correctly so that it becomes a benefit to you rather than a burden. Change then becomes a source of courage rather than discomfort. In this instance, the power of God was shown to bring peace in the midst of a natural danger that could never have been addressed without His help.

In another instance, Jesus received a message that Lazarus, a dear friend of His, was sick. Because He kept a close relationship with God the Father, Jesus knew how to handle specific times of critical change. How did He respond to this news? He didn't drop everything but adjusted His thoughts to control His response, based on the Father's guidance. *"When he heard this, Jesus said, 'This sickness will not end in death. No, it is for God's glory so that God's Son may be glorified through it'"* (John 11:4). In other words, "This change will result in a benefit." Then, Jesus stayed where He was for two more days. He continued what He was doing rather than going to Lazarus. The disciples apparently believed He was staying in order to avoid danger from His enemies. (See verse 8.) Yet it was for an entirely different reason.

Only when Jesus knew Lazarus was dead did He tell His disciples, in effect, "Okay, let's go." Why stay away while Lazarus was sick, and then go to him after he died? This seems like an immature—or, at least, confusing—response to a tragic situation. However, it was the best response to change in this instance because it was based on Jesus' purpose. Yet note that even in the midst of fulfilling His purpose, Jesus was not immune to the grief that accompanied Lazarus' death. *"'Where have you laid him?' [Jesus] asked. 'Come and see, Lord,' they replied. Jesus wept"* (John 11:34–35). This is what happened next:

They took away the stone. Then Jesus looked up and said, "Father, I thank you that you have heard me. I knew that you always hear me, but I said this for the benefit of the people standing here, that they may believe that you sent me." When he had said this, Jesus called in a loud voice, "Lazarus, come out!" The dead man came out, his hands and feet wrapped with strips of linen, and a cloth around his face. Jesus said to them, "Take off the grave clothes and let him go." (John 11:41–44)

Sometimes, people will rush toward us, or call us, and say, "Quick! Something happened to somebody! We have to go!" Some emergencies need our immediate presence. Yet others may not. Depending on the need, you may respond, "I must finish this first." Others may think you are irresponsible or unfeeling. Yet maturity sometimes requires us to say, "I understand that this has occurred, but I can't change anything right now, and I can't contribute constructively to the situation, so I must continue doing what I am doing." Each situation is different, and we must be discerning. Yet reacting with alarm and without proper thought is immature, while responding purposefully and productively is mature.

Suppose the bank tells me, "You are behind in your mortgage payment by four months, and you apparently have no immediate prospects for producing the income to pay it. We are going to have to repossess your house." Assuming the money isn't provided miraculously, and my relatives and friends don't have the funds to help me out, how should I respond to the loss of the house? How should I handle this situation in a mature way? I can't print money or rob a bank. So, I allow the bank to take the house, and I decide to go back to my parents' house for a while and live with them because they said I can live there rent-free. Even though the situation has cost me my property—and perhaps my pride—taking this action would be handling it with a mature response. An immature response would be to become depressed and then get mad at everybody, blaming the bank, Wall Street, and the rest of the world. Then, my blood pressure would go up (perhaps leading to other medical problems), I would be irritated constantly at everybody, and I'd waste time that I could be using to initiate new plans for my life. Which do you think is the better approach to that change?

Change Teaches Us the Mature Response to Unsettling Times

We've seen that change is the greatest motivator for progress and advancement in our world. This principle applies not only on a societal scale but also on an individual one. We can learn to let change move us forward in personal maturity levels, abilities, and skills. Being mature means responding to life from a mind-set grounded in the understanding that life is unpredictable. Maturity is also the constructive response to expected change.

As the writer of the letter to the Hebrews said,

No discipline seems pleasant at the time, but painful. Later on, however, it produces a harvest of righteousness and peace for those who have been trained by it. Therefore, strengthen your feeble arms and weak knees. "Make level paths for your feet," so that the lame may not be disabled, but rather healed. (Hebrews 12:11–13)

Use change in your life as you would discipline. James wrote,

Consider it pure joy, my brothers, whenever you face trials of many kinds, because you know that the testing of your faith develops perseverance. Perseverance must finish its work so that you may be mature and complete, not lacking anything. (James 1:2–4)

What is a trial? It's a change. You were doing fine, and then the doctor told you that you have a lump in your breast or prostate problems, and that announcement brought a change. When you experience change, James said, *"consider it pure joy."* Why? Not because you're immune to pain or sorrow, but because you *know* something. You know that this trial has come to test your faith, to develop your perseverance, and to make you mature. Whenever you see the word *tribulations* or *trials* in the Scriptures, the concept of maturity is always implied in the context. This is because, again, maturity is tested and manifested by change. When the unexpected happens, when adversity comes against you, your maturity will be tested.

So, remember this astute saying by the last newscaster David Brinkley: "A successful person is one who can lay a firm foundation with the bricks that others throw at him." Life will throw many bricks at you. Catch them and lay a foundation that will enable you to move a little higher. Critics are also stone-throwers. Catch their rocks and build steps. Don't allow the negative things that occur in your life to make *you* negative. Turn them into something positive and use them as a foundation for your next move.

> "A successful person is one who can lay a firm foundation with the bricks that others throw at him."

A mature person will always use adversity for advancement.

Release Your Potential through Change

Do you see what a powerful force change really is? It actually manifests who you are inside, not just what you portray to others. It will test your true level of maturity. It will challenge your traditions to see if they stand the test of time. It will make you wonder, *What can I really trust in?* It will challenge the strength of your resolve to fulfill your purpose in life. And it has the potential to train you in maturity—if you will allow it to discipline you. In essence, you can release and maximize your full potential only through change.

Through all these experiences that stretch us and cause us to grow, we can rely on our one Constant. As Paul wrote,

> *In all these things we are more than conquerors through him who loved us. For I am convinced that neither death nor life, neither angels nor demons, neither the present nor the future, nor any powers, neither height nor depth, nor anything else in all creation, will be able to separate us from the love of God that is in Christ Jesus our Lord.*
> (Romans 8:37–39)

To exist is to change, to change is to mature, to mature is to go on creating oneself endlessly.
—Henri Bergson, philosopher and winner of the Nobel Prize in Literature

Part 3

INITIATING CHANGE IN YOUR WORLD

THE MIND-SET OF A CHANGE AGENT
Attitudes for Interacting with Change

*The main dangers in this life are the people who want to
change everything—or nothing.*
—Lady Nancy Astor, first female member of British Parliament

As we initiate and fulfill our God-given purposes, we become change agents. Sometimes, our exercise of change will seem relatively independent of the transitions in our culture. We will be the ones bringing something completely fresh to our lives, to the lives of our family members, to our communities, and to our nations. At other times, our exercise of change will be closely connected to the tides of transition already taking place in our nations and the world, and we will be integrating our changes into these broader changes.

As I mentioned in the chapter "Worldwide Tides of Change," I believe there are certain groups of people who are developing as leaders in the world—people who formerly were considered perpetual followers. There is an ongoing shift in the balance of leadership influence and in the perceived value of people groups in the world. New respect and opportunities are coming to some of those from Third World nations. Change is already causing or will cause the ascendancy of people who did not hold leadership positions before. These groups, especially, must understand how to interact with times of transition.

No matter who we are or where we live, however, many of us are still getting used to the idea of *leading* change. Therefore, whether you are involved in change in a local sphere of influence or on a wider scale, you must know how to conduct yourself when change comes *through* you. You need to truly understand the nature of change and the perspectives and attitudes that are essential for interacting with it successfully.

You must have the mind-set of a change agent.

Knowledge, Understanding, and Wisdom— The "Principal Thing"

One of our greatest enemies in life is ignorance. Hosea was a prophet in Israel who delivered this message to the Israelites from God after they had rejected a knowledge of Him: *"My people are **destroyed** from lack of knowledge"* (Hosea 4:6, emphasis added). A lack of knowledge can undermine and even destroy your opportunity to fulfill your purpose.

However, what is worse than not knowing something is not knowing that you do not know it! If you are aware of your lack of knowledge, you can go about seeking to learn and understand the knowledge you need.

King Solomon wrote, *"Wisdom is supreme; therefore get wisdom. Though it cost all you have, get understanding"* (Proverbs 4:7). I also like the way the King James Version puts it: *"Wisdom is the principal thing."*

Understanding is the *comprehension* of knowledge; wisdom is the *application* of knowledge. In critical times of transition and shifting seasons, we must not only see what's happening around us but also understand the times and be able to respond to them wisely.

The historical record of 1 Chronicles describes the men of Issachar, who *"understood the times and knew what Israel should do"* (1 Chronicles 12:32). These men discerned the times in which they lived. Having understanding about situations helps us to know what to do in the midst of them. If we want to make right decisions and initiate effective action, then we must understand the seasons. Moreover, godly wisdom will allow us to oversee changing times successfully. Wisdom is the "principal thing" because to initiate positive change, we must apply our knowledge and understanding with good judgment.

As we have seen, if we lack knowledge about God's seasons in our lives, we won't be prepared to participate in them. A change agent, therefore:

> *Wisdom is the "principal thing" because to initiate positive change, we must apply our knowledge and understanding with good judgment.*

+ Is open to listening to God's Holy Spirit, who reveals seasons

+ Studies and understands the times

+ Expands his knowledge

+ Applies wisdom

Many great possibilities have been lost to the world because of ignorance. As a change agent, you have to be aware of what is happening *to* you and *through* you. You also must not be ignorant of your responsibilities during your season. Know, study, and comprehend what change means for you, and understand your responsibility to deliver what God desires you to deliver through change.

Mental Preparedness for Change

As we will discuss more fully in the next chapter, being given a purpose, in itself, does not prepare you to fulfill that purpose. Neither does the emergence of a season, alone, guarantee your participation in that season. It simply guarantees change. You have to actively prepare to engage with change, and this readiness begins with *mental preparedness.*

If we are to harness the coming season, fully participating in the purpose of God, we must make ourselves ready for our roles in it. King Solomon wrote,

> *There is an evil I have seen under the sun, the sort of error that arises from a ruler: fools are put in many high positions, while the rich occupy the low ones. I have seen slaves on horseback, while princes go on foot like slaves. Whoever digs a pit may fall into it; whoever breaks through*

a wall may be bitten by a snake. Whoever quarries stones may be injured by them; whoever splits logs may be endangered by them. If the ax is dull and its edge unsharpened, more strength is needed but skill will bring success.…Woe to you, O land whose king was a servant and whose princes feast in the morning. (Ecclesiastes 10:5–10, 16)

The above passage implies that if you promote a person to a leadership position while he still has a follower mentality—it mentions the "fool" who is put in a high position, the slave on horseback, and the king who used to be a servant—then the whole land is in trouble. Of course, this is not to suggest that someone who has been a slave or a servant should not become a leader. Rather, it indicates that someone with the *mind-set* and *habits* of a slave is not properly prepared to lead others.

Mental preparedness includes such things as (1) a solid expectation and acceptance of the inevitability of change, (2) an assurance of your worth to God, (3) a certainty of the value of your contribution to your generation as an instrument of change, (4) a decision to pursue your life vision, and (5) a determination to persevere in that vision, even if circumstances become difficult. Developing mental preparedness before you experience change is best, but if you are currently in the midst of transition and lack this frame of mind, then seek to develop it in the midst of change.

Humility in Your Season of Change

Sometimes, when we are raised up by God to bring about change in the scheme of history, we may be tempted to confuse the purpose for the change with our positions in the change. Sadly, this seems to have been the case with many change agents in their generations. They forgot they were instruments of the changes and not the Author of the changes. They should have remembered that they were, in a sense, temporary "delivery systems" for these changes.

Consider what happened to the mind-set of the Israelites over the years after they were called by God through Abraham. The point of their being chosen was very clear. When God called Abraham, He said,

Leave your country, your people and your father's household and go to the land I will show you. I will make you into a great nation and I will

*bless you; I will make your name great, and you will be a blessing. I will bless those who bless you, and whoever curses you I will curse; **and all peoples on earth will be blessed through you.***

(Genesis 12:1–3, emphasis added)

In other words, God was telling Abraham, as well as the *"great nation"* of descendents who would come through his son Isaac, "Here is My purpose for choosing you to bring about change: I want you to be a channel through which I will reveal Myself to all the nations of the world and draw people back to Me." God gave the Israelites special status, love, and protection, yet the change was not about them but about His plan for the world.

What happened? Many who were part of the chosen channel interpreted their being chosen to mean that they were superior to those whom they were called to serve. Corporately, they were meant to reveal the true God to the nations of the world who had no real knowledge of Him. The goal was to restore the people of the world to relationship with God. A conduit, or pipe, is never more important than the water. Yet many Israelites began to boast about the fact that they were chosen and to think that they were the "water" instead of the "conduit." They ended up acknowledging their purpose in name but not in reality. This is why the Pharisees were defensive about their identity when Jesus tried to show them their original, true identity, as well as the path back to God. *"Abraham is our father,"* they answered. *"If you were Abraham's children,"* said Jesus, *"then you would do the things Abraham did"* (John 8:39). Abraham had understood his role as a conduit, and he had lived accordingly. Unfortunately, many of his descendants failed to understand this role.

We must realize that seasons come to raise up "pipes" to deliver divine water to each generation. When you are an agent of change, you must never confuse being an agent with being the Author. You are temporary, you are dispensable, and you can be replaced. You have to remember that, ultimately, change is happening *through* you and not *by* you.

Suppose you are a participant in a change through which God takes oppressed people and puts them in

> **When you are an agent of change, you must never confuse being an agent with being the Author. Ultimately, change is happening through you and not by you.**

influential leadership positions. How should you interpret that change? You could think, *Well, we are now better than everybody else. It's our time for revenge and oppression. It's our time to become the masters.* This is not the appropriate nature and mind-set of a true agent of change. Like everybody else, you're just an agent. If the previous agents abused their positions, this doesn't give you the right to do the same.

God will test you to see if you will do the job He's given you. If you won't, He will give it to someone else at some point. In other words, God will never become a victim of the "pipe." His water will be delivered to the garden of earth. And He will keep searching for pipes that will serve as conduits and not pretend to be the water itself.

Just as some stewards of past seasons failed in many ways to fulfill their roles and had to be replaced, we, too, must realize that we can be replaced by the next generation or even during our own generation. Let humility, understanding, and sensitivity be trademarks of our leadership.

Unafraid of Your Season of Change

Positive change can be hindered when those who have been called to be change agents are afraid to accept—or to fully accept—that calling. I want to encourage you who are now moving forward in tides of change, who are emerging to serve God's purposes to the world, not to be afraid to accept that challenge. Embrace it as a divine obligation, as well as a human responsibility toward your fellow men. Become a faithful conduit of the grace of God, helping to fulfill His plan for your generation.

Fear of accepting one's call often stems from feelings of inadequacy and a failure to understand one's significance in the world. If you've been taught long enough that you're "nothing," it becomes almost impossible for you to believe it when someone tells you, "You are important. God created you for a purpose."

I know that this fear is real. I had to struggle with it a little myself when I first dealt with the issue as a young person and asked myself, *How important am I, **really**, to the world?* It's a tough question to answer.

When someone tells you that you can be an agent of change, therefore, it's easy to become fearful. You may say, "No, not *me*!" Yet God answers, in effect, "You are a conduit, and you can deliver something to the world that is going to touch a generation yet unborn." Remember that you are not the "water," and that God will take responsibility for the results as you serve the gift He has given you to deliver to the world.

In addition, it is natural for feelings of anxiety, uncertainty, and fear to accompany any venture we make into unknown territory. As new seasons come upon us, this common experience touches both those to whom change is happening and those through whom change takes place.

I often emphasize in such situations that whatever God calls for, He provides for. God gave you potential, ability, gifts, and talents to manage the responsibilities of a season of transition. You have the ability to be a change agent. You are capable of being a leader in your sphere of influence in this world. After you have discovered your true purpose, do not doubt your call. Rise to the task, knowing that you were designed for this moment. Let your initiation of change transform your fear into faith.

A Sense of Responsibility for Your Season of Change

A change agent does not shrink from his responsibility to his generation, whether change happens *to* him or *through* him.

Some people believe it's too late for them to become change agents—to change themselves and their environments to bring about positive transformation. There are different reasons for this outlook. Perhaps they've become discouraged and need to have their hope renewed. However, some people are intimidated by the *responsibility* of change.

Again, when seasons of inevitable change occur, you must come to terms with the reality that conditions will not remain the same, and that events are transforming life as you knew it. You have to understand that you cannot ignore, deny, or prevent change. You must actively take responsibility to respond properly to the change with the intent of participating in it and benefiting from it.

Having a responsible attitude toward seasons of change also means that you understand your obligation to serve humanity and to do your part in the Creator's good purposes for the earth. If you don't take responsibility for your season of change, you will become guilty of abandoning a divine assignment. You will have withheld from an entire generation something you were supposed to deliver to them. Your season of change is not about fame or other forms of self-gratification. It's about faithfully carrying out what you are called to do in life, for the benefit of others, as well as yourself.

A Capacity for Greatness

To sum up, the mind-set of a change agent is one that (1) seeks knowledge, understanding, and the application of wisdom, (2) is mentally prepared for change, (3) does not boast in a season of change but understands the role of a "conduit," (4) is unafraid of seasons of change, and (5) takes a responsible attitude toward change.

All peoples on earth—in every nation and of every race—must realize the capacity for greatness that lies dormant within them and develop the mind-set of a change agent. As we recognize our potential to bring about change through initiating our purposes, and as we take steps of faith in that direction, God will bring tremendous positive change to our world.

As [a person] *thinks in his heart, so is he.*
—Proverbs 23:7 (NKJV)

CHARTING YOUR COURSE TO A PREFERRED FUTURE
Essential Features of Purposeful Change

It takes a lot of courage to release the familiar and seemingly secure, to embrace
the new. But there is no real security in what is no longer meaningful.
There is more security in the adventurous and exciting, for in movement
there is life, and in change there is power.
—Alan Cohen, inspirational author

Many people think of life as a difficult thing, but it's truly a gift from God. If you approach life fearfully or antagonistically because of the reality of change, you will certainly hinder your progress. We must think of life as a privilege, not a plague. It's a blessing to be given life, and we need to handle it thoughtfully and carefully. We can do this by developing, initiating, and monitoring a plan for positive change that will help us to fulfill the Creator's purposes for our lives. Initiating change, as we have seen, is the highest form of response to change.

Your Path to Planned, Positive Change

For many years, I have been speaking to people all over the world about personal potential and leadership. I talk to people in government, in corporations, in churches—in a variety of venues. This has involved quite a lot of air travel. In recent years, making the right flight connections at the right times has become difficult because of my increasingly busy schedule.

Several years ago, an aircraft was donated to my organization, which has been a great help in my travels. It has also opened up a new world of knowledge for me. I'm naturally inquisitive—I enjoy learning what makes things function successfully—and the pilots of the aircraft have taught me a great deal about flying. When you fly on large, commercial airliners, you don't learn much about what it takes to pilot a plane. But when you are sitting right in the cockpit with professional pilots, and when you have an opportunity to watch them firsthand, you learn quite a bit.

Many times, I would sit down with the pilots and ask them questions. For example, I'd look at the panels of buttons and dials in the cockpit, and I would ask them, "What is that for? Why is that moving? What's this light?" In the process, I discovered some fascinating things about flying an aircraft. However, I was mostly reminded of some essential aspects of successfully implementing purposeful change. My conversations about piloting helped me to understand better the way our Creator works and how we are meant to relate to Him as we pursue the purposes He's given us to accomplish in life. Here are some points about piloting an aircraft and their parallels for the pursuit of fulfilling purpose.

Determine Your Destination

The first thing a pilot must do may seem obvious, but it is essential: he must determine his *destination*. You don't just take off from an airport with no destination in mind. Air traffic control has to know exactly where you're going to land *before* you take off.

Where you want to end up determines the path you choose in life—the priorities you set and the daily habits you follow.

What is your destination in life? Most people go through life without knowing where they want to end up. Yet they are still surprised when they do not arrive there. Our destinations are determined by our understanding of the purposes God has for us. Our purposes, then, determine the initiation of change in our lives, which ultimately leads to the fulfillment of those purposes. In other words, you chart your course from the end to the beginning. Where you want to end up determines the path you choose in life—the priorities you set, the practices you nurture, and the daily habits you follow.

In our piloting analogy, the Creator is air traffic control, or "the tower." Through seeking the Creator's purpose for your life and what He has placed inside you to do, you can determine your desired destination. You confirm that this is where you want to go, allowing Him to guide you all the way.

One of my favorite verses of Scripture is Proverbs 16:9: "*In his heart a man plans his course, but the* LORD *determines* ["*directs*" NKJV] *his steps.*" Who makes the plans? Man does. Who determines or directs the steps of that plan? God does. You make the plan, based on God's purpose for you, and He directs you.

If you don't have a plan, there will be nothing for God to direct you in. I wrote a plan for my life when I was thirteen years old. It wasn't written in calligraphy, and the words weren't fancy. I wrote it on a dirty piece of paper! Yet I am still doing, in some form, everything I wrote on that paper. So, don't be intimidated about the form or style of your plan. Just get it written down. Once you have written a plan, that plan will begin to grow and expand, but you have to start somewhere.

It was the plan I wrote that kept me away from drugs and alcohol when others my age were using them. The first gangs were formed in the area where I grew up, and bars were easily accessible in my neighborhood. Yet I survived those influences because I had a plan for my life. I knew that involving myself in those things would derail that plan. To protect your future, therefore, you must take this truth to heart: If you approach life casually, you will end up a casualty. Changing your life for the better won't just happen on its own. You need to actively make decisions and plan your course. You have to make specific choices that put you on a route that corresponds to your God-given purpose.

Here are some questions to ask yourself in regard to understanding your purpose so that you can determine your proper destination. It is a good idea to review these questions monthly to keep yourself focused on your preferred future.

1. Do I know where I want to go in life?

2. Do I know the Creator-inspired desires of my own heart?

3. What do I want to achieve—specifically?

4. What is my destination in life?

After you've asked yourself these questions, *can you describe your destination?*

File Your Flight Plan

Second, after a pilot determines his destination, he must file a flight plan. This means he must not only know his destination but also submit to air traffic control the *specific route* he intends to take, or the plan he has made to get him there, *before* he leaves the ground.

Do you have an idea of your destination but lack the specifics of what it will take to arrive there? In other words, have you filed your "flight plan" yet? If you approach life halfheartedly, you will miss out on your preferred future. Disappointment awaits those who merely make plans but do not implement them. You must be committed and faithful to carry them out.

What, specifically, will it take to get you from where you are to where you want to go? Map out a detailed route to your preferred future, including everything necessary to arrive there. The list may include knowledge, skills, education, research and development, financing, equipment, materials, facilities, communications tools, means of attracting interest and support, personnel, and product. Before a commercial plane takes off, airline personnel need to make sure everything about the aircraft is in working order: that it has enough fuel to make it to its destination, that it is mechanically sound, that it is properly staffed and equipped, and so forth. In a similar way, you should adapt the specifics of your plan to the needs of your particular destination, making sure your plan is in "working order." What you need for your plan won't be exactly the same as what someone else needs. If you were going on a skiing trip to Switzerland, you would pack your suitcase differently than you would if you were going on a beach vacation to the Caribbean.

Have you set a specific course to take you to your dream? What resources do you need?

Monitor Your Flight Path with the Tower

Once a pilot has determined his destination, filed his flight plan with air traffic control, and been cleared for takeoff, he can leave the ground and begin the actual flight. But he never loses touch with the tower. The pilot must frequently be in contact with air traffic control to monitor his flight plan.

In this stage of pursuing your purpose, you know where you want to go and have made a detailed plan to get there. You have left the ground of your past and are on your way to a new destination and a greater level in life. Now, you must make sure to monitor your course by remaining in constant communication with the Creator and continually reassessing your activities according to your original plan.

You must make sure to monitor your course by remaining in constant communication with the Creator and continually reassessing your activities according to your original plan.

The course you *should* be on to implement planned, positive change in your life is determined by your purpose. Yet the choices you make daily will decide the course that you are *actually* on. Perhaps your plans for change began with some resolutions. Maybe you wrote them out on a piece of paper or typed them on your computer and printed them out. You have them taped to your wall, but you haven't done any of them yet. Why? Even though you had a goal, you didn't make the necessary choices in keeping with that goal. Making a plan alone is not a guarantee that you're going to succeed. It is making good choices that will enable us to stay on course to our purposes.

Are you staying in constant communication with your Creator and continually reassessing your life choices according to your purpose?

Follow All the Instructions of the Tower

During a flight, a pilot must carefully follow the instructions of the tower because air traffic control can see the total picture of what's going on around him. One of the pilots of our aircraft explained to me, "In any given moment, within a five-mile radius around you, there could be numerous aircraft. You can't see them, but they're at different levels all around you. The tower knows where all the other planes are, and the tower knows where you are." Since the pilot doesn't know where he is in relation to all those planes around him, he has to depend on the tower to guide him, doing everything the air traffic controllers tell him to do.

Similarly, God knows about every single situation surrounding you. You have to stay close to Him and follow His instructions every day, through reading His Word and through prayer, because you don't with whom you could be in danger of colliding.

God will give you a resilience that comes from trusting in His Word. Sometimes, He will tell you to hold steady when you want to move, or vice versa. One time, when we were in flight, I heard the captain say, "Oh, no." That didn't sound good. I asked, "What happened?" He said, "They want us to pull back. We have to slow down." I said, "Man, we're late." He said, "But the tower says we have to slow down." I repeated, "We're going to be late." He said, "Yeah, but the *tower* says...." The pilot didn't listen to my opinions about the situation; he listened only to the tower. After about twenty minutes, he told me air traffic control had sent a message saying that he could speed up again. When the plane began to gain speed, we suddenly saw a large commercial airliner whoosh by, and he said, "That's why they told me to slow down." We had been in its path.

As we seek God, He will sometimes tell us, in effect, "Hold it right there," but we're impatient and want to pursue something. Yet, again, He sees the big picture, including the hindrances and dangers involved with moving forward too quickly. For example, God may warn you, "Don't marry this person," and you may say, "God, You don't understand. I love this man!" God will still indicate to you, "Don't do this." He knows there's another man about two miles away on a different latitude, and he's the right one. But since you can't wait, you move ahead too quickly and end up in an emotional collision. Or, you end up with a helicopter rather than a Boeing 747! Again, we have to follow God's guidance completely because He can see the whole picture, whereas we can't.

Are you following God's guidance for your life?

Stay Steady On Course, Unless Redirected by the Tower

At times, as we were flying, the pilot would switch to a different frequency on his radio, allowing us to hear pilots from various commercial airlines talking to one another. A few times, when we were listening to the other pilots, we would hear one of them say, for example, "There're some thunderstorms up ahead. It's bumpy up here." Another pilot would add, "Yeah, at twenty thousand feet, it's bumpy." Still another would report, "At forty thousand feet, we've got thunderstorms." However, the pilot of my plane couldn't change course based solely on what the other pilots were saying. Even though we heard that storms were up ahead, we had to go by the word of the tower, because the tower guides the aircraft's course (except, perhaps, in a complete emergency), and it can see the storms in relation to where the plane is.

There are times when everything around us, or everything in our own lives, seems to be falling apart. Yet if we're listening for our Tower, we will be able to hear God say, "Keep believing and stay steady." Maybe you've lost your house, but God says, "Still believe." The very business God told you to start closes its doors, but He keeps saying, "Stay steady." You lose everything you thought was already yours, but God says, "Keep on course." When things change and conditions are chaotic around you, you have to obey the last command God gave you. It may be something you were supposed to do but failed to carry out, and it needs to be set right.

Several years ago, I heard a wise statement by a Nigerian bishop: "We should never be selective in obedience." Selective obedience is deciding to obey some things but not others. You can't do that when you're following God. You have to obey the Tower, no matter what He says. As an illustration, during a flight on our airplane, the pilot will sometimes tell me, "We have to go up another two thousand feet." When I ask why, he'll say something like, "I don't know, but they say we must go up. Our altitude has to change two thousand feet." Then, he might say, "Okay, now we have to go down; we have to drop another ten thousand feet." Again, if I ask why, he will say, "I don't know; the tower says it, so we just have to do it." In other words, whether he understands the reason or not, he needs to do whatever the tower tells him to do.

God sees the big picture, and He knows how to help you avoid the obstacles or storms up ahead. Do you listen to God like that? Once more, He sees the big picture, and He knows how to help you to avoid the obstacles or storms up ahead. He knows what potential collisions or "enemy attacks" are in your "airspace," and He can see the whole "weather system" within range of your life. So, He may say, in effect, "Go down ten thousand feet." You answer, "God, I don't see anything. It looks good up here!" But He says, "Drop right now. Drop your association with this person, or you're headed for trouble. He has charted a destructive course." "But, God, we went to school together!" "Drop down." "But we go way back." "Now!" God is trying to preserve your future—and, perhaps, your life. How many people have failed to fulfill their potentials because of unhealthy friendships? Many who are struggling with destructive habits right now were encouraged by their friends to start them.

What are you doing right now that is taking you off course? What should you be doing right now that you aren't doing? Whom are you listening to that you shouldn't be listening to? Think about it: If you are not in the place you should be, you may make it hard for others to fulfill *their* futures. On the other hand, don't allow others to miss their best futures because you were in the wrong place along with them, encouraging them in something that wasn't right for them. Bad environments destroy good destinies. Nothing can destroy the fulfillment of your purpose faster than being in the wrong environment. So, check your physical, emotional, mental, and spiritual environments. Staying on course will protect both you and others. We'll discuss more about how to get back on course in another chapter.

In addition, if you aren't accomplishing what you wanted to, perhaps it's because you've listened to other "pilots" around you who were telling you their perspectives on the ways things are, what you can expect, and what direction you need to go in. Good counsel from those who have proven trustworthy is important, and it should be heeded. Yet you may receive advice from well-meaning people that is not appropriate for you. You have to be careful when listening to other people's experiences because they are not necessarily God's will for your life. If you're trying to accomplish something, they may tell you what they've been through and how tough it was for them to try to do the same thing. You can listen to them, but ultimately, you must listen to the voice of God, because He may be doing something different in your life.

After Moses died, and Joshua became the leader of the Israelites to take them into the Promised Land, God told Joshua, *"As I was with Moses, so I will be with you; I will never leave you nor forsake you"* (Joshua 1:5). Yet when you read about Joshua's experiences in the Promised Land, you notice that God worked in his life in ways that were different from His ways with Moses. God wasn't telling Joshua to expect Him to do things in exactly the same way. He meant that His *presence* and *power* would be with Joshua continually, in everything he did, as long as he stayed close to his "Tower." God also said to Joshua,

> *Be strong and very courageous. Be careful to obey all the law my ser-*
> *vant Moses gave you; do not turn from it to the right or to the left, that*
> *you may be successful wherever you go. Do not let this Book of the Law*
> *depart from your mouth; meditate on it day and night, so that you may*
> *be careful to do everything written in it. Then you will be prosperous*
> *and successful.* (Joshua 1:7–8)

Are you staying steady on course, following God's leading, whether or not you understand it right now?

Watch Your Landing!

It's been said that more aviation accidents take place during takeoff and landing than while planes are in the air. As a concluding parallel to our piloting analogy, therefore, let me encourage you to pay extra attention when you are completing your plan. We talked earlier about making sure you know your destination before you take off. Without a clear goal, you can "crash" before you really begin, or you can end up way off course.

Yet you can run into trouble just as easily by becoming complacent just before "landing." To use another transportation illustration, people often get into car accidents a short distance from home. Since they are almost at their destinations, they lose their concentration on the road. They may become too relaxed or start thinking of what they'll do when they arrive home. They are distracted, and they end up in collisions of some sort.

When you think you are about to accomplish your plan, make sure you guide it all the way to your destination, remaining alert to any final directions from your Tower, wrapping up any unfinished details, and addressing any problems that might prevent your "landing gear" from working. Then, if everything is in place to land, you will fulfill your God-given purpose, successfully enacting the positive change in your life or in the lives of others.

It takes a quality choice to make an effective change.

Remember that it takes a quality choice to make an effective change. If you make that quality choice in the beginning and follow through all the way to the end, the desired change will become a reality.

Life is a progress, and not a station.
—Ralph Waldo Emerson, essayist and poet

OVERSEEING CHANGE IN YOUR WORLD
Keys to Planning and Preparing for Change

He that never changes his opinions, never corrects his mistakes,
and will never be wiser on the morrow than he is today.
—Tryon Edwards, theologian and descendant of Jonathan Edwards

I n chapter one, I described various ways people react to change. The first two reactions were that people (1) watch change happen, and (2) let change happen. You have the option of doing nothing while change happens to you, or you can *make* change happen—even in the midst of inevitable transition or of negative change that you can't prevent from occurring. *You* can determine whether you will initiate change to improve your life or merely allow your circumstances to undermine it.

The Paradox of Choice

In the chapter "The Mind-set of a Change Agent," I introduced the idea that being *called* to a purpose, in itself, does not *prepare* you for that calling. You must put certain things in order in your life to get ready for it.

In other words, *you have to choose your chosen destiny.* I call this decision the "Paradox of Choice."

The decisions and plans related to my purpose that I committed to as a young teenager set the course of my life on a positive path, one that I continue to follow in fulfilling my purpose and serving others in my generation. Other young men my age who were brought up on the same street as I went on a completely different path—and the results were also completely different. The only difference between the direction in which I went and the direction in which these other young men went were the changes that we initiated based on our *decisions.* Our decisions created our unfolding futures—distinct futures. Therefore, even though you may understand that transitions occur and environments change, *you* must decide the kinds of positive change you will introduce into your own life.

We know that not all change is improvement. Yet without change, there can be no improvement. If you want to improve, you have to alter something in your life. Again, the fact that God gave you birth to do something significant doesn't mean you're automatically going to accomplish it; you have to choose what He has chosen.

Will you actively choose the purpose God has given you?

Established but Not Guaranteed

Our challenge is that our destinies are *established,* but they're not *guaranteed.* Let me give you an illustration of this fact. I paid the tuition for my daughter and son to go to college. But whether they graduated was up to them, not me. My "destiny" for them was already established, and I was committed to paying their college fees. In my mind, I'd already seen them with their degrees at the end of their university studies. But, would they make it to the completion of their purposes? To do so, they had to go to classes, pass exams, complete projects, and fulfill all the school's requirements. And my daughter and son did graduate from college. (Now, they both also have their master's degrees, so they took that purpose even further.)

God operates in a similar way. He has already established your end, but whether you make it there requires your participation. Our Creator doesn't obey Himself for you, write down plans for you, or develop skills for you. Every human being is given a free will, and this is why we must make the *decision* to choose our chosen destinies and to do what is necessary to fulfill them. We are not animals, which live on instinct. We are human beings who direct our lives based on our decisions. Therefore, even though God has a good plan for your life and knows what He wants you to accomplish, it is up to you to plan your course, to make life changes that will move you toward it, and to stay on course, as we saw in the previous chapter.

> *Though God has a good plan for your life, it is up to you to make life changes that will move you toward it, and to stay on course.*

Ordered Change

Like the men of Issachar, if you see that the times are shifting and that you must soon take responsibility in the midst of a specific change, then you have to prepare for it.

> *The steps of a good man are ordered by the* Lord, *and He delights in his way. Though he fall, he shall not be utterly cast down; for the* Lord *upholds him with His hand.* (Psalm 37:23–24 NKJV)

Unless we plan ahead, our lives will be in disorder when change comes. The Lord God desires to order our steps and to uphold us. Therefore, order your plans according to your God-given purpose. Follow through with a mind-set of preparedness and act in ways that will enable you to be ready for the demands of change. Develop skills and abilities that will qualify you to be a change agent. Don't wait for the change to come first, or you will likely be overwhelmed by it. This will expose your lack of understanding in regard to your purpose, as well as your lack of readiness for change.

The following are four practical keys to overseeing change in your life that will allow you to plan and pursue your purpose. They apply to both change that is already occurring around you and change that you are anticipating will arrive.

Four Keys to Overseeing Change

1. *Study the trends and demands of change.* This key relates to gaining knowledge, understanding, and wisdom so that you may develop the

qualities of a change agent. Suppose you become aware that significant change is happening, or you begin to see certain trends occurring in your nation or culture. Start to analyze the implications and impact that will result from this change. Also, consider how this change could relate to other changes that may naturally follow it.

Particularly study the problems in your environment that were created by the change. It could be that part of your purpose is to creatively address one or more of those problems. If you determine that this is the case, you can develop a strategy to use your gifts and abilities to address and solve those problems.

Let's look a little closer at the times in which the men of Issachar lived. We know they were able to read the change in their nation, as well as the meaning and impact of that change. The setting for their "understanding of the times" is the period after the nation's first king, Saul, had been chosen by God—and after Saul had gone so far away from God's purposes that he needed to be replaced as leader. The men of Issachar perceived that God had rejected King Saul in favor of the young David, and they went to join David. The Scriptures say they *"knew what Israel should do"* (1 Chronicles 12:32).

Whoever can read seasons of change and be prepared to act on them will be a leader. The clan of Issachar was large and had many men who were able to fight. Yet it was not their size or strength that made them truly powerful. It was their capacity to understand the times in which they lived. They knew what was happening in their environment, they could interpret the conditions, and therefore they could project for the whole nation what it should do.

Such insight gives a person *proactive* power. This is the reason why receiving prophecy from God was so important in the context of the national life of the Israelites. Prophecy is, in one sense, a preview of coming change for the purpose of preparing for it.

Let us look at an incident when Jesus and His disciples were at the temple in Jerusalem.

Some of his disciples were remarking about how the temple was adorned with beautiful stones and with gifts dedicated to God. But

Jesus said, "As for what you see here, the time will come when not one stone will be left on another; every one of them will be thrown down."
(Luke 21:5–6)

Jesus went on to tell His disciples that they would be persecuted, and that Jerusalem would be besieged. He talked about it with certainty, as if it had happened already. He did so because He knew it was coming, and He warned His disciples about it so that they could prepare and be proactive in the midst of it. He also told them,

Look at the fig tree and all the trees. When they sprout leaves, you can see for yourselves and know that summer is near. Even so, when you see these things happening, you know that the kingdom of God is near.
(Luke 21:29–31)

Jesus was saying that just as we are familiar with certain signs in nature that correspond to specific seasons, we should recognize the signs of the times. This analogy brings us back to our need to study the trends of change that occur around us. Do not be ignorant or apathetic toward your environment, but be alert to what is going on and what impact it will have.

2. *Plan and prepare for change.* After studying the trends of change, begin to prepare a specific plan to address them. Your strategic plan should include practical projects and programs you intend to initiate, such as developing new skills, in anticipation of the change. You can also decide if any modifications need to be made to your immediate environment that will enable you to respond effectively to the impact the change will have on you. For example, what alterations to your lifestyle and reordering of your financial commitments might need to be made in response to these trends?

Your strategic plan should include practical projects and programs you intend to initiate, such as developing new skills, in anticipation of the change.

When change is already directly affecting you, it's too late to plan ahead for it. Yet you can develop plans to address what you perceive as the next, obvious, impending change that is coming as a result of the present change. In this way, you can learn to prepare continually for change.

3. *Position yourself for change.* Positioning yourself for change means putting your plans into action. Take personal responsibility for energizing your potential, developing your skills, and otherwise refining yourself for maximizing the benefits of the change that is coming or is already happening to you.

Positioning yourself for change also means continually managing all your resources closely—including your time, your relationships, your money, and your other assets—in such a way that you stop any hemorrhaging of their value and usefulness, which will be detrimental to the stability of you and your family during the change.

Make any other alternations that are necessary, even though they may be temporarily difficult, to safely come through a challenging change that is ushering in your season and enabling you to progress toward fulfilling your purpose.

4. *Change on purpose.* In the next section, I've listed some specific ways in which you can plan and position yourself for change after studying the trends of change. Yet this fourth point, "Change *on Purpose*," is the overarching key and deciding factor in overseeing change in your life. Changing on purpose means making a decision always to be, to the best of your ability, on the front curve of change.

In this way, you are not pushed by change but propelled by your purpose. You initiate ordered change for the benefit of yourself and your environment, facing times of transition with optimism, energy, and personal involvement.

Seven Essential Ways to Plan and Prepare for Change

1. *Change your knowledge base.* Pursue information that equips you to deal with an environment in transition. This may mean reading relevant books and other literature, taking a seminar or a course, or even going back to school.

People who change careers have to become familiar with new perspectives and a new realm of information. Likewise, as you sense changes in your nation, community, or personal life, study the knowledge you need to effectively address these changes and benefit from them.

2. *Change your skill sets.* Gain skills that enable you to address the challenges that change presents. In the process, identify and review your natural gifts, then develop skills related to them that will enable you to better pursue your purpose.

We must make certain that we clearly understand the difference between a gift and a skill, or we may not apply ourselves diligently to developing the skills we need:

+ Skill is not a gift from God.

+ Skill is not inherent at birth.

+ Skill cannot be obtained by osmosis.

+ Skill cannot be transferred or inherited from others.

+ Skill can only be learned and developed.

Ecclesiastes 10:10 says, *"If the ax is dull and its edge unsharpened, more strength is needed but skill will bring success."* Therefore, improve your skills. Pursue the training necessary for your role in the next season of your life. Other people cannot do this for you, even though they may be able to give you advice regarding avenues that will help you to develop certain skills. We must realize that, ultimately, *we* have to initiate our own skill development.

3. *Change your library.* In the process of changing your knowledge base and developing new skills, you may need to invest in some resources—for example, books, workbooks, and DVDs—as well as utilize other media, such as podcasts, in order to prepare for and properly respond to change. Perhaps your personal library contains only novels. While everyone needs some downtime and relaxation, you can branch out from those novels and read books that will enable you to learn and grow in preparation for, and in the midst of, change.

4. *Change your associations.* Sometimes, responding effectively to change will require you to make new acquaintances and to enter a new circle of associates. For example, you may need to join a club, a professional network, or a community organization.

In order to address a time of transition in your life, you may also find yourself needing to adjust the levels of your relationships. You may not be able to spend the same amount of time with certain people as you used to, and you may need to increase the time you spend with others. Be sensitive to your longstanding friendships but also to the fulfillment of your purpose and your need to address significant change in your life.

If we fail to prioritize what is important to us, we will be carried off by the currents of life and not accomplish our purposes.

5. *Change your priorities.* Change has a way of making us adopt new priorities. First, as we have seen, inevitable change sometimes forces us to give up certain relationships, as well as aspects of our lifestyles and habits. Moreover, in order to be successful in pursuing our purposes, we can't be involved in *everything* but must be selective in how we spend our time and what activities we choose to participate in. Proactively changing our priorities means choosing carefully how we live our lives rather than just letting life happen. If we fail to prioritize what is important to us, we will be carried off by the currents of life and not accomplish our purposes.

6. *Change your expectations:* We can never omit this vital facet of addressing change! Remember, what protects us from disappointment and frustration in regard to change is the expectation of change. We will often need to adjust our expectations in response to new changes we experience because there is always some area of our lives in which we've settled into the anticipation that it will remain the same.

Perhaps you fully expected to receive a raise from your company, but now, people are being laid off, and you have to withdraw your expectation, at least for a time. Or, maybe you fully intended to pursue a certain vocation, and change has blocked that path. Your expectations for your life have to be altered. However, remember that your purpose remains the same. Therefore, you must now discover how to fulfill your purpose under different expectations and avenues or find out how you should live your life until that door reopens in the future.

7. *Change your spiritual focus.* Times of transition and change can help us to realize that we have not pursued vital spiritual priorities in our lives. In order to center on what is most important, we must discover and practice spiritual habits that will help each of us to develop a relationship with God and grow in that relationship.

For you, changing your spiritual focus may include realizing that only through faith in Jesus Christ can you begin to have the relationship with God He desires you to have with Him.

Perhaps you have never read the Bible or read it only occasionally. Now, as you face the challenges of change and energetically pursue your life's purpose, you realize you need to know God's Word. You understand that you must learn how to live according to spiritual values and principles, which are higher than those of the physical realm. In this regard, even though you may never have attended church before, you now recognize the importance of fellowshipping with a circle of people who are spiritually minded.

If you have already developed a relationship with God, changing your spiritual focus may mean spending more time praying and meditating on what you read in the Scriptures so you may be open to receiving fresh ideas from God about how to prepare for change and how to deal with current change. We tend to allow our busy lives and the "crisis of the moment" to shorten the time we spend with God, yet these are the times when we need Him the most.

The Power of Decision

The decisions you make about your life will direct your unfolding future. You can introduce positive change by ordering your life according to your God-given purpose. Apply the keys to overseeing change and commit to specific ways of positioning yourself to address change.

Remember that your destiny is established but not guaranteed. *Will you choose your chosen destiny?*

I am prepared to go anywhere, provided it be forward.
—David Livingstone, missionary, medical doctor, and explorer

WHEN YOU NEED A COURSE CORRECTION

It's Never Too Late to Change

Change does not necessarily assure progress,
but progress implacably requires change.
—Henry Steele Commager, historian and author

Even after we've made a decision to initiate change in our lives, there may be times when we move off course—to a greater or lesser degree. What is important during these times is that we not become discouraged and convince ourselves that we "knew it would never work out" and "it isn't worth trying anymore." It is vital that we not *stay* off course but immediately make a course correction to move back in line with our purposes. As the quote at the beginning of this chapter emphasizes, if we truly want to make progress in life, we must persevere in implementing change.

Let the Creator Decide

One of the saddest things I've heard from people over the years is, "I cannot change." Have you convinced yourself that you cannot get back on track because you have wandered from your purpose—and from God? We owe it to ourselves—and our Creator—to wholeheartedly pursue the purposes He's given us. When we go back to our original visions and tap into who we are and what we're meant to do, we will become reenergized to move forward in positive change.

Whether you've never "taken off" and are still idling on the runway or have gone off course mid-flight, it is *never, ever* too late to change. Think of Abraham, the great patriarch. At seventy-five years of age, he was approached by God with an unusual proposal:

> *Leave your country, your people and your father's household and go to the land I will show you. I will make you into a great nation and I will bless you; I will make your name great, and you will be a blessing....To your offspring I will give this land.*   (Genesis 12:1–2, 7)

Even at Abraham's advanced age, travel of this nature might have seemed plausible. But there was another problem with this scenario: he was childless. The suggestion that his "offspring" would inherit the land was ridiculous in light of his situation. Yet God didn't think it was too late for Abraham to make a major move and to father a child through whom an entire nation would come—especially since that child wouldn't be born for another twenty-five years!

If we give up too soon, we might overlook or prevent the arrival of important vehicles of change in our lives.

This is why we need to let the Creator make these decisions instead of us. If we give up too soon, we might overlook or prevent the arrival of important vehicles of change in our lives. Abraham could have told God, "It's too late for me." He wouldn't have hindered anything too important—only the beginnings of the nation of Israel! Note that his choice wasn't a private decision— it significantly affected history. We shouldn't presuppose that our decisions to initiate change affect only us. Nelson Mandela came out of prison when he was over the age of seventy and became the president of South Africa. I wonder how many times he thought, while he was sitting in his cell, *How old will I be when I get out? I will be useless.* I'm glad he didn't say, "It's too late for me to change. It's too late for me to lead a country and help a people."

"I Have Considered My Ways"

We have to take an honest look at where we are in relation to the purposeful changes we want to make in our lives. Are we on course, or have we taken a detour? Most of us know the courses we are on. We know our daily habits. In our hearts, we know exactly what we're doing and where we're headed.

For example, if you keep going to work late and making the boss angry, you know your future—for your job, anyway. If you don't exercise and eat right, you know what course you're on in terms of your health. If you're lying about your relationships or about certain things you shouldn't be doing, you know that you will hurt others—and yourself. Do you want to stay on the same unproductive or counterproductive course you have been on?

Earlier, we talked about the analogy of piloting a plane in regard to pursuing our purposes. Proverbs 14:12 says, "*There is a way that seems right to a man* [pilot], *but in the end it leads to death* [collision]." Perhaps the way you've been living seemed right at one time, or you wanted it to be right, but it's led to a collision or a dead end. Sometimes, people think they can outsmart God. They say, "I'm not going to do what I need to do, but I'll still be able to fulfill my purpose." You can't get away with shortcuts—or substitutes. Trying to substitute something else for God's plan for your life is like trying to run your car on orange juice instead of fuel. It may run for a little while on the little bit of gasoline that is left in the tank—but then the juice will hit the carburetor. Likewise, you may think you have been doing fine. But the juice hasn't hit yet.

Psalm 119:59 says, "*I have considered my ways and have turned my steps to your statutes.*" The writer of the psalm was saying, in essence, "I've thought about the way my life was going, and therefore I have changed course." The first thing you do is to "consider your ways"—look at what you're actually doing and where your actions are leading you. "*I will **hasten and not delay** to obey your commands*" (verse 60, emphasis added). Make a course correction right away. If you know where you want to end up, recalculate and turn in the right direction.

Here are some questions for "considering your ways":

+ Am I truly satisfied with the course I'm currently on?
+ Is the course I'm on enabling me to fulfill my purpose?

+ What took me off course, and what has kept me there?

+ Is how I'm spending my time contributing to my vision? Is what I'm doing in secret taking me to my purpose?

+ Have I been deterred or distracted from my course? If so, what happened? What disrupted my life that has taken me off course for weeks, months, or years?

+ Why am I in the same condition that I was in last year, with no improvements? Why haven't I developed or advanced in any areas?

+ Does what I'm doing have eternal value?

Unless you address these questions, your life will remain the same. You'll keep doing things that cause you to diverge from the path to your purpose. Recommit to your vision and then keep your word to *yourself* that you will do what it takes to fulfill it.

To help you answer the above questions as you evaluate your life, here are some reasons and circumstances to consider that indicate you may need a course correction.

Reasons for Changing Course

1. *You missed your goal.* You didn't accomplish what you planned because you didn't pursue wholeheartedly what you wanted to achieve. Your course correction involves going back to your original flight plan to accomplish your purpose.

2. *You know that your present actions are detrimental to your life and purpose.* If what you're doing is causing you problems, you have to change your course and do *different* things that will put you a clear path to your purpose. For example, perhaps you fell into debt because you slipped into unwise financial habits. Make a course correction by developing a plan to get out of debt and follow sound financial practices.

3. *You need to eliminate friction.* Sometimes, you need to adjust your course because the direction in which you're going seems filled with friction. Once, I was talking with a young man whom I knew had gotten engaged, and I asked him how he was doing. He said, "Fine." I said, "Are you married yet?" He said, "We've been engaged for a while,

but we keep fighting." I saw that he wanted to talk about it, so I said, "Tell me about it. What's the problem?" He said, "Every time we think things are working out, we have a big fight. We've been fighting for a year." So, I said, "Let me give you some advice. Every relationship has problems, and all relationships have conflict. Conflicts are normal. But if you keep fighting, you need to evaluate the *source* of the fights before you get married. For example, if you keep having conflict because she's jealous about the young women you work with, and every time she sees you talking with another woman, she gets angry, then the source of the conflict is jealousy. If your job requires that you work with a variety of people, both men and women, and she can't handle that, then that tells you what your future marriage will be like." After such advice, someone may say, "Yes, but I believe the Lord is going to change [him or her]." If your boyfriend or girlfriend isn't willing to change to *win* you, then he or she won't be willing to change to *keep* you. The Lord may have been trying to change him or her for a long time, but He can't change a person if he or she is not willing to change. The same person may say, "But I *know* [her or she] will get better." "Oh? How long have you been going together?" "Twenty years." You get the picture.

4. *You must change your altitude (attitude).* Sometimes, the necessary course correction involves a change of attitude. Again, what if God, in His purposes, takes you from a top position in your company to a new job where you have a lowly position? Can you adjust to that "altitude" change and have a good attitude in the midst of it? This might be a case in which the change of job is necessary in order for you to have a break-through of some sort in your life. Joseph was put in prison unjustly before he was promoted to ruler. It's very important to have positive perspective, even when you feel as if you're in "prison." That position may help you to mature because it will reveal negative inner attitudes that need to be dealt with. Or, you may find your new position to be better for you physically and emotionally. Because you no longer have to work overtime, you can spend more time with your family. When you come through this change by achieving what God wants for you there, you will have been refined and prepared for a new leadership role—wherever you are.

5. *You experience unexpected disruptions.* When life unfolds in a way you didn't expect, you might be thrown off course for a short time, but then you need readjust to get back on course. This disruption might be a minor inconvenience or a large setback. Either way, don't allow it to bump you permanently from your flight path.

6. *You need to work through a "detour."* Sometimes, we experience major crises in our lives or have disastrous personal failings. I want to encourage you that even though you have stumbled or fallen, you can still make it to your destination. If you have failed, you will need to ask God for forgiveness and seek reconciliation with those whom you've hurt. Working through such detours means you must take a revised route in order to get back to the main flight path—but you will get there. "I didn't plan to be in such financial straits." God says, "That's okay—stay on course." "I didn't plan to get a divorce—again." God says, "Stay on course!" "I didn't count on my baby dying!" God says, "Take time to grieve, receive My comfort, and don't give up hope! Keep pursuing your purpose." Every setback or failure can be transformed into a testimony. God will turn things around, and you will be able to grow from it and tell others how you developed faith and strength in the midst of it. Whatever you're going through right now, you will go *through it*—and come out again on the other side. If you learn and grow from it, you're going to come out better than you were when you went in.

7. *Your timing is off.* Sometimes, we may mistake the timing of our seasons and try to act too soon. If the time is not yet right for certain things to occur, you must regroup and make a course correction that will prepare you for the time when the season is ripe for harvest.

8. *You displaced your values.* Displacing crucial spiritual and moral values will always throw us off course. The following are some areas we particularly need to evaluate in our lives to make the necessary course corrections.

   + *Changed priorities.* You have to reevaluate your current priorities. For example, whenever you start replacing God with other things, your future is in trouble. Perhaps, instead of valuing God, you've fallen in love with material things. You used to make God your priority, but now you have two jobs and are running a business, and you've stopped going to church regularly. What do you value most in life? Do you value being famous? Do you value the pursuit of money? Do you value being known as a success? After answering these questions, ask yourself, *What is of eternal value?* Also, what friendships and associations take priority in your life, and which are you pursuing? Are they beneficial to you? Sometimes, our professional or social relationships become more important than our family relationships or accountability relationships, and so we've strayed off course. It's vital that we give top priority to our relationships with God and our families.

+ *Familiarity with God and abuse of His grace.* Sometimes, we can become so "familiar" with God that we don't think we need Him; we're not even interested in Him anymore. We think we already know everything there is to know about Him and the Bible. When we take God and His grace in our lives for granted, however, we abuse our relationship with Him. We may begin to take it too casually when we think, say, and do things that are contrary to His nature and will. Then we wonder why our lives are off course!

+ *A lack of personal time with God.* Perhaps you used to get up early in the morning and spend time praying and worshipping God, but no longer. What happened? You're off course because you've found more "important" ways to spend your time. As a result, there has been little or no spiritual growth in your life. You may still be pursuing your purpose, but you feel empty about it. It's time to check in with your "Tower." My personal time with God is the most important part of my day. I enjoy God because I *choose* to make Him a priority every day. If you don't spend time with God in prayer, you won't receive the spiritual refreshing you need, and you will be beaten down by life. You will struggle and become frustrated. Don't let your work become more important than worship. Check your values. Check your activities. Don't pursue *things* at the expense of God.

+ *A lack of time in God's Word.* When you lose your love for God's Word, you often lose your love for God Himself. And when you lose your love for God, your whole life changes for the worse. That's when you start altering your priorities. So, you see, one detour leads to another. You start valuing other people and things more than your Creator, and they become your gods. Suddenly, your life no longer represents God's true nature and ways, and He seems to walk away from you. I am committed to reading the Bible because I want to stay on course. The Bible says that if you will seek God, you will find Him. (See Jeremiah 29:13). But if you don't seek Him, He'll hide Himself from you. (See Deuteronomy 31:17.) It is sad to say, but many times, it takes a crisis for us to come back to God when we've grown apathetic toward Him.

+ *Unhealthy personal relationships.* You may need a course correction because you've been spending time in the wrong company. As I wrote earlier, some of our so-called friends are working against us by persuading us to take up habits and practices that are destructive, which short-circuit our visions for our lives. *"Blessed is the man who does not walk in the counsel of the wicked or stand in the way of sinners or sit in the seat of mockers. But his delight is in the law of the* LORD*"* (Psalm 1:1–2). Are you "sitting" with others, as if in agreement, when they scoff at God? Perhaps you have moved away from your close relationship with God because you started dating someone who isn't interested in Him and doesn't want to go to church with you. When a relationship pulls you away from God, you have gotten off course, and you should make an immediate course correction. If this person doesn't value your highest priority, he or she doesn't deserve to be with you. Just because someone is good-looking doesn't mean he or she is right for you. Of course, you need to end a relationship immediately if it is leading you out of your marriage. You should also evaluate your professional associations. Where are they taking you? You may say, "Well, it comes with the job." You have to set standards that won't cause you to compromise your priorities. You don't sacrifice your relationship with God for a job. If you're spending time with people who will turn you from Him and your purpose by encouraging negative attitudes, behaviors, and habits, it's time to recalibrate your relationships.

+ *Entertainment instead of personal growth.* This is often a significant problem, but most people don't even think about it. They will spend hundreds of dollars on concerts or DVDs that are not really helpful to them, but they won't put any money into something that will enable them to grow spiritually, intellectually, or emotionally. They will spend hours amusing themselves but little or no time developing their potentials.

This Is Halftime

Any of the above scenarios may describe your life right now, but God has brought you to this point in time to give you an opportunity to make a course correction for your life. Let's use another analogy related to getting back on course: "halftime."

Every football game has a halftime—a break of about twenty minutes to a half hour when the teams are allowed to go back to their locker rooms, rest, and revise their strategies. If a team hasn't been playing well, the coach will give the players specific pointers for how they should adjust their approach. Perhaps the other team was tougher than they expected and they became distracted and forgot the original game plan.

Similarly, you've been on the field of life. You haven't been living well or making progress toward your vision, but this is your halftime. Consider me as your life coach right now, and remember that God's Spirit is always with you as your Counselor, so make sure you listen to Him.

Here's my halftime talk: "Look, you've been losing a lot of yardage, and you're in danger of losing the game. So, this is what you need to do: remember your original game plan, stick to it, and keep a positive attitude. Don't dwell on your mistakes but correct them."

When players receive this type of instruction during halftime and take the coach's advice, they go back on the field as a revitalized team. They are on the right course, they are energized—and they start putting points on the scoreboard.

Remember our discussion of times and seasons? Time allows us to have "halftimes" and "time-outs" to regroup. Paul wrote, *"Be very careful, then, how you live—not as unwise but as wise, making the most of every opportunity, because the days are evil. Therefore do not be foolish, but understand what the Lord's will is"* (Ephesians 5:15–17).

We are to make the most of every opportunity. Maximize your life as you've never done before.

When you reach a certain age, the above verse becomes even more important to you because you recognize that you don't have any more time to experiment with life. I made a decision that every appointment I make and every opportunity I invest in to has to be connected to my purpose and God's will for my life. If people want to change, I will help them. If they want to improve, I will dedicate my time to them. But, if they just want to waste time, then I have to decline. I am committed to spending my time with others who *do* want to pursue their purposes. We are to make the most of every opportunity. Maximize your life as you've never done before. Make every day count. Don't be foolish, but use your time effectively.

Keys to Course Correction

Let us now look at some keys that will help you to make your course correction. If you are twenty-five years old or younger, you especially need to take these keys to heart—because there is even greater pressure on you to get off course than there is for those who are older. Again, they know well that time is limited—and that no one stays twenty-five forever!

1. *Review, revise, and reset your vision.* If you want to make a course correction, reexamine your God-given purpose, or what you want to become. What did you want to do with your life? What is your preferred future? How should your vision be refined to make it more specific or clear for you to follow?

2. *Assess your obstacles.* Evaluate the things you need to overcome in order to get back on track and achieve your goals. Again, you first have to acknowledge the truth about where you are currently headed. Which areas, above, did you recognize about yourself and your life? Be honest about any ways in which you are setting up your life for collisions. Then, list specific steps you will take on order to get back on course.

3. *Study the failures of others.* Let other people's negative examples teach you. Evaluate the lives of people in the Bible, people you have heard about, and people you know personally who have strayed from their courses in life. Note the effects on them. Then, ask yourself if you are

following in their footsteps. You aren't so different from them, and you will also fail if you keep making poor choices and avoiding the good things that you should be doing.

4. *Commit or recommit to good counsel and accountability.* When you keep following the same advice from the same people and find yourself coming up with the same bad results, something needs to change. Who are your counselors? To whom are you listening? To whom *should* you be listening? Discover those who will give you good counsel and ask them to help you evaluate your life and your plans for pursuing your purpose. Find someone with whom you can pray, and tell that person, "I'm going to give you my plan for the year on paper. I want you to help me make sure I keep it." Commit to having someone be your coach and accountable relationship—someone whom you give permission to ask you, "Are you doing what you said you wanted to do? Are you being faithful to yourself?" We all need this type of help and encouragement.

5. *Cut off relationships that are hazardous to you.* In order to maintain a strong relationship with God so you can fulfill your life's purpose, you may need to sever some relationships right away. Review the above points about unhealthy relationships and misplaced priorities to help you evaluate this area of your life. Then, take the necessary steps to free yourself from these negative influences.

6. *Change the environments of your life that are hindering your progress.* Negative life environments might include the forms of entertainment you engage in, your current job situation, your associations, and your habits—especially the secret ones. If they're hindering you, you must eliminate them. Then, create new, positive environments through which you can follow your priorities and experience personal growth.

7. *Look for **God's** detours.* "*No temptation has seized you except what is common to man. And God is faithful; he will not let you be tempted beyond what you can bear. But when you are tempted, he will also provide a way out so that you can stand up under it*" (1 Corinthians 10:13). God promises to give us a "*way out*" during times of temptation so that we may resist them or hold up under them. If you're going to stay on course or make the proper course correction, you must take the "escape routes" that God shows you. For every temptation, He will always give you a

way out. Take it! When you sense God saying such things as, "Leave now," "Don't call him," "Don't answer the phone," or "Don't go there," listen to Him!

Let Your Choices Change Your Course

Even when you think you're on course, take time out periodically to review, renew, revise, and refocus your flight path, as necessary. Again, ask yourself, *Am I going the way I want to go? Am I becoming the woman or man I committed myself to be? Am I doing things that will cause me to develop into the person I want to become?*

The course you are currently on will affect your whole life. If you need to make a correction, take courage and do so.

The course you are currently on will affect your whole life. If you need to make a correction, take courage and do so. Don't let a crisis change your course; let your *choices* change your course. Receive all the blessings, possibilities, and opportunities God wants for you. The past is history. Today is the beginning of your future.

Progress is impossible without change, and those who cannot change their minds cannot change anything.
—George Bernard Shaw, author and playwright

TEN WAYS LEADERS RESPOND TO CHANGE

Change Is Inevitable. Change Is Necessary. Change Is Possible.

Change in all things is sweet.
—Aristotle, Greek philosopher

Pursuing our purposes transforms us into change agents. What is a *change agent*? It's another term for *leader* or *emerging leader*. Whoever can read seasons of change—in his or her own life and in the world at large—and be prepared to act on them will lead others.

Leaders must understand the principles and benefits of change because leaders have a major influence on the overall environment, conditions, and attitudes of those who are participating with them in fulfilling their visions. Many people refer to such participants in vision as *followers*. I don't often use this term because (1) it limits people's mind-sets about what they can be and do, and (2) it doesn't reflect that fact that each person is meant to fulfill his or her own purpose within the context of the wider vision in which he or she is a participant.

Let me be clear that, by *leaders*, I am not referring only to those whom many people traditionally think of as leading, such as CEOs, presidents, managers, and supervisors. Here is my definition of leadership, which I have developed after decades of researching and studying leadership, as well as training thousands of individuals who have aspired to leadership:

Leadership is the capacity to influence others through inspiration, generated by a passion, motivated by a vision, birthed from a conviction, produced by a purpose.

Leaders Initiate Change By and On Purpose

Change agents exercise leadership in their particular spheres and environments of influence.

The above definition crystallizes what we have been discussing in part 3 of this book, "Initiating Change in Your World." Leaders initiate change *by* and *on* purpose. Change agents exercise leadership in their particular spheres and environments of influence, whether in the home, classroom, community, church, nation, business, youth group, fraternity, or civic organization—in all realms of life. In this context, all of us as leaders must understand that how *we* handle change will influence what happens in the lives of those who are invested in our visions, as well as how they themselves perceive change.

Do you remember, as a child, being frightened about something? You probably looked to your parents for reassurance. If they seemed calm about the situation, you became calm about it, too. If they looked worried or anxious, you remained feeling unsettled.

When we become adults, we are able, through maturity and experience, to absorb or deflect situations that used to frighten us. However, people still often look to those who seem "in charge" for feelings of assurance during major events, such as national emergencies, natural disasters, war, or the death of a national figure.

If someone in a leadership position seems disoriented or overcome by change, this reaction often spreads to the whole environment of the group or organization. If there's one thing that leaders must be distinguished by, it is their capacity to respond effectively to change for the sake of those whom they're leading, as well as for themselves.

The leader almost always confronts change first. The most important work of leadership, therefore, is the ability to handle constant confrontation with change, as well as to initiate change. Leaders are moving constantly. They are taking people *to* change, *through* change, *to* change again.

Change is also the incubator of leadership development. Through learning about, experiencing, and analyzing change, leaders discover the nature of change, the potential of change, the necessity of change, the power of change, the impact of change, the benefits of change, the challenges of change, and the hazards of change.

Change Is One of a Leader's Greatest Assets

It is impossible to lead without change, so change is one of a leader's greatest assets. The success or failure of any leader may be measured by how he or she responds to, oversees, and benefits from change.

Every nation and organization, as well as every individual, must cultivate the ability to respond effectively to change because none of us exists in a vacuum. Even the most unassuming organization or nation will be forced to confront change at some point. Being hesitant or passive in such situations may lead to the end of that organization or nation.

This is why groups, companies, and countries, like individuals, must engage in campaigns of self-development. Research and development departments in many businesses are designed to ensure continuing innovation and implementation of change for the betterment of the company. In the life of an organization or business, success requires periodic reinvention, as we saw in the example of the Swiss Watch Company. John Walter, former president of AT&T, said, "When the pace of change outside an organization becomes greater than the pace of the change inside the organization, the end is near."

In both personal and corporate life, then, leadership is ultimately about *change*. In this last chapter, I would like to summarize ten ways in which leaders respond to change, briefly highlighting essential principles and benefits of change that we have covered throughout this book.

1. Leaders Expect Change

Leaders are aware that change is a principle of life. In leading others, they know that they are going where they have never been before and that the passage to this "new land" is change. Leadership is about "relocating" individuals, organizations, businesses, communities, or nations to a future destination. The leader must help those who are invested in his or her vision to embrace this change in order to move toward the desired goal.

Leaders are also aware that nothing is permanent except God and His promises. This means that they must live in continual expectation that things could change at any moment, and be mentally prepared for this inevitability, while trusting in God as their "constant."

2. Leaders Initiate or Create Change

It is impossible to lead while…

+ staying where you currently are.

+ maintaining what you have.

+ assuming that someone else will initiate change.

+ expecting someone else to tell you what to do.

+ waiting for the future.

A true leader…

+ provides the vision of a preferred future.

+ initiates a change of direction.

+ sets a change of pace.

+ encourages participation in reaching the goal.

The leader leads by creating the next step toward the future. He or she develops the process and the programs that produce the changes necessary to move toward the desired end.

Remember that, in the Scriptures, there is no record that God ever performed a miracle in the same way twice. Following in this creative pattern, leaders constantly exist in "the now" rather than staying in the past and create new things.

3. Leaders Interpret Change

It has been said that what really matters is not what happens to you but what you do about what happens to you. This is the mentality of true change agents. Leaders always seek to analyze and interpret changes in their environments from the perspective that all change contains within it opportunities that are beneficial to their purposes and causes. In essence, they always seek the good in every situation.

> *What really matters is not what happens to you but what you do about what happens to you.*

4. Leaders Guide Change

After analyzing and interpreting change for its benefits, leaders then actively seek to direct that change in their lives—whether the change is created by the leaders or has been imposed on their environments—for the advancement of their purposes.

5. Leaders Plan and Design Change

Leaders create strategies that are regulated by their visions in order to take their groups or organizations to the futures they aspire to.

A leader is a leader because he or she has already visited the future in his or her mind and has returned to the present to take others there. Leaders do not just stumble into the future; they *plan* their way there. Since the future demands change, leaders must design the series of changes that are necessary to make their ways (and others' ways) to the preferred future.

God warned the Egyptian pharaoh through a dream, which Joseph interpreted, that Egypt was about to experience some changes—seven years of plenty followed by seven years of famine. What did Joseph do? He *expected* it, and so he *planned* for it. In the years of plenty, he put grain aside to be used in the seven years of famine. He protected himself, his family, and his adopted nation against change.

6. Leaders Prepare Themselves for Change

After accepting the responsibility and embracing the obligation of a God-given assignment, the leader makes the necessary changes in his or her spiritual life, personal life, professional life, educational life, and social life, and develops the skills required for the journey.

7. Leaders Are Inspired by Change

The unique distinction of leaders is that they do not panic in an atmosphere of unexpected or expected change or chaos. Rather, these conditions provide an incentive to inspire the leader by testing his or her resolve, capabilities, potential, creativity, and spiritual reserves.

Men and women of courage have the audacity to believe God even in the midst of seemingly impossible situations. These leaders are convinced that *"with man this is impossible, but with God all things are possible"* (Matthew 19:26).

8. Leaders Grow through Change

True leaders understand that every challenge is a classroom and every experience is a lesson. Therefore, they embrace the unknown or the unexpected as opportunities to learn new lessons and to expand their experiences. Change initiates discomfort, which leaders use for the sake of advancing their lives.

9. Leaders Benefit from Change

True leaders always use the unexpected, the unplanned, and the unanticipated events, circumstances, and situations of life to their advantage. They have learned to maximize misfortune for the advancement of their noble causes.

10. Leaders Exist for Change

The very purpose and essence of leadership is to move from the known to the unknown in order to improve life and to create something better for others. You cannot "lead" to a place where you already are. Therefore, leadership is created by, motivated by, sustained by, and exists for, *change*.

I would like to leave you with these thoughts:

+ Change is inevitable.
+ Change is necessary.
+ Change is possible.
+ Change is here.
+ What will *you* do with change?

> *Change is inevitable. Change for the better is a full-time job.*
> —Adlai E. Stevenson II, politician and U.S. Ambasador to
> the United Nations

PRINCIPLES FOR EMERGING LEADERS
A New Approach to Life

A man may fulfill the object of his existence by asking a question he cannot answer, and attempting a task he cannot achieve.
—Oliver Wendell Holmes Sr., physician and author

I have written this section of the book for all those who find it especially difficult to believe they can initiate positive change in their own lives. It is for *you* who, even now, don't fully accept the idea that you can be a leader in your realm of gifting and influence, and that you can become a change agent in the midst of a world in transition.

You may come from a family or a society that has told you—for whatever reason—that you will never amount to anything. Or, you may be awakening for the first time to the idea that you can take the initiative in your life rather than just let life happen to you. This may be true especially if you or your ancestors grew up under slavery, colonialism, or another form of institutional oppression, such as Communism, and you seem to have inherited a mind-set of oppression that holds you back in life.

Regardless of your background, I want to encourage you to do what you never imagined was possible: take steps toward your preferred future. The statement by Oliver Wendell Holmes Sr. quoted above could describe me when I was a young person growing up in the Bahamas. I kept asking myself, *Why can't we have new Third World leaders? Our lack of national leadership is destroying us.* That persistent question eventually created Bahamas Faith Ministries International, my leadership seminars, and the Third World Leaders Association. I asked a question that I couldn't answer and attempted a task that I couldn't have achieved if I had followed the traditional mind-set modeled around me.

> *Do what you never imagined was possible: take steps toward your preferred future.*

This is the time for you to take on a new mind-set and a new approach based on the positive benefits of change. I consider you an *emerging leader*. The changes that you initiate, and your response to the changes that are taking place in the world, will enable you to release your potential. Here, then, are principles for emerging leaders to help you to fulfill your purpose in life.

Emerging Leaders Interpret the Past with Insight

The first principle for emerging leaders is to interpret the past with insight. Often, those who doubt that they can initiate positive change are dealing with troublesome issues and attitudes stemming from their pasts. Yet we have seen that God can transform even the negative experiences of our lives into beneficial outcomes.

We are the products of our histories, as well as how we integrate those histories into our lives. While we don't want to be chained to our pasts, we need to understand them in order to appreciate the present. With all the challenges that we face, we must gain a God-inspired vision of a positive future—not just for our lives in eternity, but also for our lives on earth now.

Consider the Past as Prelude—Not as Your Present

When God called Moses to free the Israelites from slavery in Egypt, Moses was hesitant. He said, "*O Lord, I have never been eloquent, neither in the past nor since you have spoken to your servant. I am slow of speech and tongue"* (Exodus 4:10). Moses felt that his past difficulties in speaking before others disqualified him for his assignment from God. But God had a different perspective regarding who Moses was—and who he *could* be. *"The* LORD *said to him, 'Who gave man his mouth?...Is it not I, the* LORD? *Now go; I will help you speak and will teach you what to say'"* (verses 11–12).

Unfortunately, Moses held on to his interpretation of the past. He may have thought, *I haven't been able to speak well in the past; therefore, I will **never** be able to.* He thought that his past and his present were synonymous.

> *Moses said, "O Lord, please send someone else to do it." Then the Lord's anger burned against Moses and he said, "What about your brother, Aaron the Levite? I know he can speak well. He is already on his way to meet you....You shall speak to him and put words in his mouth; I will help both of you speak and will teach you what to do."*
>
> (verses 13–15)

Moses' perspective prevented him from accepting what God desired for him. Even though God eventually used him tremendously in freeing the Israelites, Moses could have experienced even more freedom and fulfillment if he had believed God's words immediately and trusted God to help him to speak without having to use his brother as a go-between.

You can think of yourself in connection with your past failures and the negative experiences you have had, or you can trust God to transform your life and give you a positive future. Remember Isaiah 43:18–19: God said, *"Forget the former things; do not dwell on the past. See, I am doing a new thing! Now it springs up; do you not perceive it?"*

The Scriptures describe the deep grief Naomi experienced when her husband and adult sons died while the family was in Moab to escape a famine in Israel. With no husband or sons, Naomi and her daughters-in-law had no means of support and were in a precarious position. Naomi had been away from her hometown of Bethlehem for many years, yet she decided there was no choice but to return there to live. When she and one of her daughters-in-law, Ruth, a Moabitess, returned to Bethlehem, her former neighbors asked, *"Can this be Naomi?"* (Ruth 1:19). Apparently, her grief and hard life had taken a toll on both her appearance and her attitude.

Naomi replied, "*Don't call me Naomi….Call me Mara*" (verse 20). *Naomi* means "pleasant," while *mara* means "bitter." Naomi allowed bitterness to characterize her life to the extent that she identified it as her name.

Naomi's life was transformed, however, as she recognized the hand of God at work in her life. God had brought her and Ruth to a place where they attracted the attention of Naomi's godly, kind, and wealthy relative, Boaz. Naomi told Ruth that Boaz was one of their closest relatives and that he could redeem the family from their distress. She advised Ruth on how to conduct herself with Boaz. Boaz married Ruth, and they had a son named Obed. *Obed* means "serving" or "worshipper." His name may reflect Ruth and Naomi's gratitude to God for delivering them from their distress.

> *The women* [of Bethlehem] *said to Naomi: "Praise be to the* LORD, *who this day has not left you without a kinsman-redeemer. May he become famous throughout Israel! He will renew your life and sustain you in your old age. For your daughter-in-law, who loves you and who is better to you than seven sons, has given him birth." Then Naomi took the child, laid him in her lap and cared for him. The women living there said, "Naomi has a son." And they named him Obed. He was the father of Jesse, the father of David.* (Ruth 4:14–17)

If Naomi had continued to live in bitterness instead of recognizing the provision and blessing that God was making possible through Boaz, she might never have experienced God's unfolding grace in her life. Moreover, by advising Ruth, she participated in bringing about a purpose of God that was much larger than the individual lives of Naomi, Ruth, or Boaz—the establishment of the family line through which David, the great king of Israel, would be born. And it was through David's line that the promised Messiah would come.

A negative past does not cancel out the possibility of a positive future, especially when we seek to recognize God at work in whatever situation we might find ourselves in. As Paul wrote, "*And we know that in all things God works for the good of those who love him, who have been called according to his purpose*" (Romans 8:28).

> *A negative past does not cancel out the possibility of a positive future.*

God Can Bring Good Even out of Oppression

Many people have difficulty interpreting their pasts in light of God's purposes because they or their ancestors experienced institutionalized oppression, and they don't see how any good could come out of that. Slavery and colonialism have left a mark of discouragement and unused potential on the lives of many Third World peoples. Let us briefly consider these effects.

Generally speaking, when the colonial powers spread into the New World, they gained control over various people groups that already had their own cultures. They would come to a land, settle in it, make it their own, and use the land for their profit. For example, they gained wealth by developing tropical lands that had good climates for growing tobacco, sugar, and cotton.

As the European powers exerted their influences across the globe, they took many West African people as slaves, placed them on ships, brought them to America and the West Indies, and sold them to European and other settlers to work on farms and plantations. Many of these settlers became prosperous, but their prosperity was not shared with the slaves. As a result, an entire segment of the population of these nations was excluded from the benefits of the societies they were helping to create. The legacy of this discrepancy of social and economic justice continues to trouble the countries that perpetuated slavery.

Yet, as deplorable as the institution of slavery is, I believe God used it for His purposes—and can still bring good out of it in the lives of the descendants of slaves. Why do I believe this? First, let us read what Paul said to an audience at Athens:

> From one man [God] made every nation of men, that they should inhabit the whole earth; and he determined the times set for them and the exact places where they should live. God did this so that men would seek him and perhaps reach out for him and find him, though he is not far from each one of us. (Acts 17:26–27)

God ultimately decided where people groups would live and where nations would develop and be established. The Scriptures say He did this for a specific purpose: *"so that men would seek him and perhaps reach out for him and find him."* God's desire is for people to seek Him and find Him, and He places them in positions where they can come to know Him.

Next, read what God said through His prophet Isaiah:

This is what the LORD says: "The products of Egypt and the merchandise of Cush [the dark-skinned race], and those tall Sabeans—they will come over to you and will be yours; they will trudge behind you, coming over to you in chains. They will bow down before you and plead with you, saying, 'Surely God is with you, and there is no other; there is no other god.'" (Isaiah 45:14)

European nations instituted the slavery of dark-skinned people in the seventeenth century, but I believe God *permitted* this to happen in order to bring them to a place where many of them could come to know Him. Remember the caravan that took Joseph to Egypt, and what Joseph told his brothers? *"You intended to harm me, but God intended it for good to accomplish what is now being done, the saving of many lives"* (Genesis 50:20).

Many Africans who were taken as slaves came from backgrounds of voodoo and spiritualism. I think that one of the reasons why God allowed slavery was so that these Africans would be removed from that dark environment of spiritualism. While slavery is contemptible, and the slave traders and slave owners had selfish motivations, many slaves who were brought to America—or their descendants—came in contact with the gospel there. They came to know the living God—which is true, spiritual freedom.

Emerging leaders, therefore, must learn to interpret the past with insight. If you—or your ancestors—were mistreated, you have a choice of continuing to curse that domination and cruelty. Or, you can discover the benefits that came out of it. We should continually work to eliminate oppression wherever we can. Yet I suggest that we should also look for the ways in which God might be using it in our lives and others' lives to move us toward His ultimate purposes. This is what it means to *interpret* change. It means to recognize the bigger picture of what is happening in the midst of that change.

To interpret change means to recognize the bigger picture of what is happening in the midst of that change.

Moreover, note how Jesus taught us to respond to oppression:

You have heard that it was said, "Love your neighbor and hate your enemy." But I tell you: Love your enemies and pray for those who persecute you, that you may be sons of your Father in heaven. He causes his sun to rise on the evil and the good, and sends rain on the righteous and the unrighteous. If you love those who love you, what reward will you get? Are not even the tax collectors doing that? And if you greet only your brothers, what are you doing more than others? Do not even pagans do that? Be perfect, therefore, as your heavenly Father is perfect.
(Matthew 5:43–48)

Love your enemies, do good to them, and lend to them without expecting to get anything back. Then your reward will be great, and you will be sons of the Most High, because he is kind to the ungrateful and wicked. Be merciful, just as your Father is merciful. Do not judge, and you will not be judged. Do not condemn, and you will not be condemned. Forgive, and you will be forgiven. Give, and it will be given to you. A good measure, pressed down, shaken together and running over, will be poured into your lap. For with the measure you use, it will be measured to you.
(Luke 6:35–38)

Wherever you're planted, therefore, determine to grow there. Don't complain, just grow. Find your purpose and move with it into the future. Don't focus on the past, because you can't change the past. There is a time and a season for every purpose. (See Ecclesiastes 3:1.) Leave behind any sense of oppression that has been like a heavy cloud hanging over your life and become all that you were created to be.

Emerging Leaders Invest in Others

Each season brings unique opportunities that we must make full use of whenever we can. When the seasons change, we have to recognize the signs and make the necessary transitions. King Solomon wrote,

He who gathers crops in summer is a wise son, but he who sleeps during harvest is a disgraceful son.
(Proverbs 10:5)

If you have been reluctant to enter into your season of change, it is time for you to start moving and gather the harvest. For example, there was a season when God used mainly foreign missionaries to bring His Word to Third World nations. I thank God for working through these missionaries. Yet those of you who were once mission fields have come to a crossroads. The season has changed. Now, God wants *you* to impact your own nation, as well as other nations, with the gospel and not just be the recipients of it. The same concept applies to all areas of life.

Unfortunately, it is often easier for people who have been oppressed or who have been told that they would never amount to anything to continue to receive from others rather than learn to give of themselves. Yet, if you merely keep on receiving, you will never become a blessing to those who need *you* to invest in *them*.

There is an important truth that says, "Success without a successor is actually failure." If missionaries leave a country without raising up nationals to carry on the work after they're gone, they have failed. On the other hand, the responsibility for success or failure also falls on the shoulders of these nationals. Some people don't want to mature and take responsibility for themselves, but they cannot afford to have this attitude.

Investing in Others Requires Maturity

We can be emerging leaders only if we are willing to develop in maturity. Let's look at the example of the Israelites, who were enslaved by the Egyptians for four hundred years. Oppressed by cruel taskmasters, the Israelites prayed to God, in effect, "Set us free from all our troubles, Lord." The Scriptures say, "*God heard their groaning and he remembered his covenant with Abraham, with Isaac and with Jacob. So God looked on the Israelites and was concerned about them*" (Exodus 2:24–25).

In response, the Lord called Moses and appointed him to release His people from bondage. After God struck the land of Egypt with a series of plagues, the pharaoh relented and let the Israelites go. Moses led them out of Egypt and into the desert, where they were vulnerable and totally dependent on God.

The Israelites enjoyed a period of time at Elim, "*where there were twelve springs and seventy palm trees, and they camped there near the water*" (Exodus

15:27). Then, they had to move on, and they came to a place called the *"Desert of Sin"* (Exodus 16:1). Sounds like a wonderful place, doesn't it? And what a contrast to Elim! It was barren, and no food seemed available there. The Israelites lost the sense of purpose they had felt at the time of their deliverance from Egypt because they focused on only their immediate problem. They said to Moses and Aaron, *"If only we had died by the Lord's hand in Egypt! There we sat around pots of meat and ate all the food we wanted, but you have brought us out into this desert to starve this entire assembly to death"* (Exodus 16:3).

To me, the Israelites were saying, "Moses, you have forced us to grow up! Why did you do that?" They had prayed for freedom for four hundred years, and when they finally got it, they wished they had died in slavery!

The Israelites quickly grumbled when faced with adversity. That sounds like many of us. We don't like independence because freedom costs too much. It requires dealing with issues and problems that others have taken responsibility for previously—even if we didn't like the way they handled them. People who have been in bondage often begin to fear freedom when it means they are required to mature.

God wants us to understand that we can mature under His guidance—and that maturity involves trusting Him to take care of us. Likewise, He wanted the entire nation of Israel to trust Him totally. He miraculously provided manna from heaven—a unique food that *"was white like coriander seed and tasted like wafers made with honey"* (Exodus 16:31)—as well as quail. Later, He provided water from a rock after the Israelites had moved on and come to a place without a source of water. (See Exodus 16:4–17:6.) Yet, even with all that God had supplied for them, the Israelites continued to doubt His goodness, power, and provision.

We can progress in deliverance and freedom only when we make a decision to grow in maturity, trusting God for His provision as we step out in faith and leadership.

Investing in Others Requires Taking Responsibility

Eventually, the Israelites reached Canaan, the land that God had promised them through Abraham and Moses. Moses sent twelve spies throughout Canaan to bring back a report about the land. Ten of the spies delivered a bad report that disheartened the people. The Israelites actually rebelled against entering their Promised Land and made plans to return to Egypt! They wanted to go backward, not forward.

> *That night all the people of the community raised their voices and wept aloud. All the Israelites grumbled against Moses and Aaron, and the whole assembly said to them, "If only we had died in Egypt! Or in this desert! Why is the Lord bringing us to this land only to let us fall by the sword? Our wives and children will be taken as plunder. Wouldn't it be better for us to go back to Egypt?" And they said to each other, "We should choose a leader and go back to Egypt."*   (Numbers 14:1–4)

When Moses and Aaron heard this, they fell on their faces before the community. Joshua and Caleb, who had also spied out the land but returned with a good report, tore their clothes and tried to encourage the people with these words:

> *The land we passed through and explored is exceedingly good. If the* LORD *is pleased with us, he will lead us into that land, a land flowing with milk and honey, and will give it to us. Only do not rebel against the* LORD. *And do not be afraid of the people of the land, because we will swallow them up. Their protection is gone, but the* LORD *is with us. Do not be afraid of them.*   (Numbers 14:7–9)

The Israelites were given solid counsel. Yet they not only rejected this counsel, but they also talked about killing Joshua and Caleb! (See verse 10.)

People sometimes reject clear purpose and direction from God if they are afraid of what might happen or don't want to take responsibility for doing their parts. The Israelites wanted to possess the Promised Land, but only in their own way—without the requirement of taking responsibility by exercising faith during difficult circumstances. God forgives our irresponsibility when we sincerely ask Him to, but our disobedience to Him can still have consequences. If we don't learn to take responsibility for our seasons now, we will suffer for our lack of faith and inactivity, and we may cause others to suffer, too.

God became angry at the Israelites for their contempt of Him and their lack of faith in His provision. When Moses asked God not to destroy the Israelites, God answered,

> *I have forgiven them, as you asked. Nevertheless...not one of the men who saw my glory and the miraculous signs I performed in Egypt and in the desert but who disobeyed me and tested me ten times—not one of them will ever see the land I promised on oath to their forefathers. No one who has treated me with contempt will ever see it.*
>
> (Numbers 14:20–23)

Taking on new responsibility in our lives involves stepping out in faith while trusting in God's love and provision for us. If we don't take responsibility, we will remain the same as we always have been. And if we remain the same, we will not fulfill our God-given purposes. This will leave us and future generations without the benefit of our initiated change—and, perhaps, without hope for the future.

Results of Remaining Merely a Receiver

What can we conclude about those who shrink back from their callings to be change agents with a vision to impact others? What happens if you remain where you are?

1. You don't have to lead—but you'll always be led.

2. You don't need to make decisions—but they will be made for you.

3. You don't have to provide for yourself—but your needs will be met on others' terms.

4. You'll become attached to traditions—but you won't learn to think for yourself.

5. Your irresponsibility will have consequences—not only for yourself, but also for others.

Are you more concerned with receiving or with giving? A self-centered approach to life may be satisfying for a while, but it lacks the true fulfillment of maturity, love, and sacrifice. Paul, one of the greatest change agents the world has ever known, quoted these life-changing words of Jesus to the elders of the church in the city of Ephesus:

In everything I did, I showed you that by this kind of hard work we must help the weak, remembering the words the Lord Jesus himself said: "It is more blessed to give than to receive." (Acts 20:35)

Emerging leaders should work for the benefit of others rather than for personal gain. Will you enter into that blessing by giving to others? Will you take responsibility for serving your nation and ensuring a positive destiny for your children's children?

You must go beyond deliverance from whatever type of trouble or oppression you have endured in your life. You must decide to move from *deliverance* to *freedom*, from the desert to Canaan, because freedom is your destiny—freedom to participate in God's ultimate purpose of drawing human beings back to Himself.

Emerging Leaders Understand Their True Potentials

Sometimes, we hold back from moving into the stream of change that God is directing us toward because we doubt our own capabilities. I have seen this mind-set firsthand in my work with Third World leaders. Despite some improvements in conditions and a greater measure of freedom and independence, many Third World peoples still grapple with issues of identity and self-worth. In part, this is because some industrialized nations have reinforced—by their attitudes, policies, or legislation—the notion that Third World peoples lack the potential, intelligence, and sophistication necessary to be on an equal plane with them. This terrible misconception has limited many talented people who have not been allowed to maximize their potentials. Another part is people limiting their own potentials because of ignorance, fear, or, again, a lack of a sense of responsibility. The potential of *all* peoples—in Africa, Latin America, the Caribbean, and Asia, as well as in industrialized nations—is abundant and cannot be measured by the negative opinions of others. Neither can it be measured by a lack of wealth or a low social status.

I want to encourage you that you possess the ability to develop, produce, create, perform, and accomplish the ideas and gifts that God has placed within you. He created you with all the potential you need to fulfill your purpose in life.

Emerging leaders, therefore, are those who have come to understand their true identities and potentials in God and to develop those potentials. The opinions of others should never determine *your* self-worth. Neither should a false opinion of yourself determine your self-image. Your identity is not found in the prejudgments of others or even of yourself but in the Source from whom you came: God, your Father and Creator. Jesus came to restore you to your rightful position in God and to reveal to you the awesome potential that is currently trapped inside you.

Emerging Leaders Develop Their True Potentials

The wealth of potential within all those who are living below their capabilities must be recognized, harnessed, and maximized by them. Are you willing to commit yourself to tapping into your own rich potential? Are you willing to help promote the creativity and productivity of the other citizens of your country? Are you willing to improve upon the outmoded, institutionalized systems you inherited from past generations, whether those systems are in government, business, education, or the church? For example, the church in the Third World should realize its potential to develop indigenous artistic works, resource management, financial autonomy, and accountability.

We must be careful not to inhibit our potentials for charting new courses for the future by being preoccupied with our pasts. We need to deposit the wealth of our potentials in this generation so that the next generation can build its future on our faithfulness to become all we can possibly be. Just as there is a potential plant or tree in every seed, there is a potential new world within your world. Remember that whatever God calls for, He provides for. Therefore, you must be committed not only to recognizing your potential, but also to developing it.

I believe it is the nature of Third World peoples to be hardworking, dedicated, and highly sensitive. Yet, as we have seen, many have developed a spirit of dependency and a lack of self-confidence. The debilitating system of colonization often provided a colony's subjects with basic training for service—but not for *productivity*.

In essence, people were taught how to grow sugarcane but not how to make sugar; they were taught how to grow cotton but not how to make cloth. Even after they became free of colonial control, they were often left in possession of significant raw materials but no knowledge or skills to transform these materials into end products.

Because they were left with the zeal of freedom but not the ability to develop viable products in the world marketplace, many Third World nations still experience financial hardship, along with an uncertain sense of identity. Moreover, sometimes, *political* colonialism has been replaced with a form of *economic* colonialism. For example, I have noticed that Third World nations still look to industrially developed states to measure their standards of quality and excellence. This can breed a sense of disrespect and suspicion about their own products while denying the tremendous potential that lies dormant within their own creativity and talents.

Yet a fresh wind is blowing through many developing countries, stirring a sense of destiny and purpose in the hearts of people. This awakening is being felt in all arenas: political, social, economic, and spiritual. With a renewed commitment to the Creator, Third World peoples must look for their inner strengths and develop the potentials lying deep within them.

Likewise, all men, women, boys, and girls of every nation and of every race need to develop their potentials and refine their skills. We have to recognize our abilities to imagine great things—and take action to make them realities. Emerging leaders know that...

1. Followers can become leaders.

2. Learners can become teachers.

3. Former mission fields can become missionaries.

4. Receivers can become givers.

Emerging Leaders Understand True Freedom

My last point—still a vital one—is that emerging leaders must recognize the nature of true freedom.

What is true freedom?

We gain our views of freedom from a number of sources, such as conversations with family members and friends, books, television, the Internet, and other media, as well as cultural, institutional, or religious traditions.

For the sake of clarity, therefore, I want to give you a working definition of freedom that I believe corresponds with the biblical perspective of freedom. First, however, let's take a look at what freedom is *not*.

What Freedom Is Not

1. Freedom is not the absence of chains or other physical restraints. In fact, freedom is not the absence of restrictions in general.

2. Freedom is not "owned" by anyone. This element of true freedom is perhaps more difficult for people to comprehend than any other. We often have the mistaken idea that *other* people are in possession of our freedom and are withholding it from us.

3. True freedom can never be given to you. (The natural inference from the previous statement is that if other people do not possess our freedom, then others cannot bestow freedom on us, either.)

Freedom has very little to do with one's external environment.

This list of what freedom is *not* challenges many traditional standards for evaluating freedom. For instance, if I confine you to prison and throw away the key, that does not necessarily mean I have taken away your freedom. Freedom has very little to do with one's external environment.

When you go to someone else to receive your freedom, as if that person can grant it to you, you have just given him or her control over your existence. This has been the single greatest misconception and weakness of my brothers, according to race, who struggle with the civil rights issue. To paraphrase Paul, I have great sorrow and anguish in my heart because of the continued cultural and spiritual oppression that is imposed upon them by certain civil rights leaders. (See Romans 9:1–3.) My heart's desire and prayer for all people is that they be delivered from the destructive belief that the government and other human sources hold the keys to their deliverance.

Under the slave trade, slaves were often made to wear chains on both their hands and feet. Those chains were psychologically transferred to their descendants by intimidation and racist propaganda. Many people continue to transfer those psychological chains to their children.

When you allow members of a particular group to bestow upon you what they think your "civil rights" or freedom should be, you greatly increase your vulnerability to bondage and exploitation in the future. Again, if you presuppose that someone has the power to extend *rights* to you, you have just given that someone the *right* to control you. Nobody should ever be given the privilege of ascribing worth to you. If you receive your value from someone else, that person can determine how much worth you have.

Many of the world's people—in every nation, culture, socioeconomic condition, and political situation—endure lives of daily drudgery. Even in highly developed, industrialized countries where wealth and affluence are more accessible, millions of citizens experience depression, despair, anxiety, and emptiness. They realize that possessions, fame, status, and power can never replace a personal sense of purpose and significance. Meanwhile, many people in Third World nations do not have access to the material possessions that industrialized cultures use as their standards of wealth and success. This contributes to their frustration and despair over their lives. Neither of these groups is living in true freedom.

The Source of True Freedom

What is the true freedom that we need?

In defining true freedom, we must first identify its source. The real issue is not "civil rights" for all but *human rights* for all. Human rights are inherent in God's creation of human beings, whereas civil rights are merely man's opinion of what human beings should be and have.

> *Human rights are inherent in God's creation, whereas civil rights are merely man's opinion.*

According to the Word of God, freedom cannot be given. If we don't understand our rights and privileges in God, they will be abused and, many times, lost to us. As God said,

My people are destroyed from lack of knowledge. (Hosea 4:6)

Jesus taught how we can experience the reality of authentic freedom. He dealt with this subject eloquently and simply. If you understand His definition of freedom, you will experience instantaneous liberty. Jesus' definition of freedom supersedes all other discourses on the subject. Other than the Bible, which is God's Word, no book can make you free. Neither can any earthly government give you self-worth. No man-made authority can give you freedom. Jesus declared,

> *If you hold to my teaching, you are really my disciples. Then you will know the truth, and the truth will set you free.* (John 8:31–32)

True freedom is the result of *understanding and receiving the truth about yourself and other people in relation to your creation in God and your redemption in His Son, Jesus Christ, as they are revealed in God's Word.* This is why people who are truly free can never be bound. Freedom is a personal discovery of the truth about God and about yourself from the God who created and redeemed you. Thus, freedom is not *bestowed* on us. We *embrace* it.

This is why the civil rights movements of the world have deteriorated into sophisticated mental and economic oppression. Freedom cannot be declared in a speech or through legislation; rather, it is personally discovered by the heart and spirit of each individual.

As an emerging leader, you can lead other people only as far as you have gone. We remain in bondage when we are ignorant of what has been provided for us through the life and death of our Lord and Savior Jesus Christ. Emerging leaders understand their own freedom in Christ and therefore are able to set others free to discover and maximize their full purposes and potentials.

Nothing splendid has ever been achieved except by those who dared believe that something inside of them was superior to circumstance.
—Bruce Barton, author, U.S. Congressman, and advertising executive

NOTES

Chapter 8, "Worldwide Tides of Change"

1. Thomas Catan, "Spain's Bullet Train Changes Nation—and Fast," *Wall Street Journal*, April 20, 2009, http://online.wsj.com/article_email/ SB124018395386633143-lMyQjAxMDI5NDIwMDEyODAzWj. html.

2. Sam Roberts, "The New Face of America: By 2042, Minorities Will Make Up the Majority of the U.S. Population. What Will This Demographic Sea Change Mean?" *New York Times Upfront*, September 22, 2008, http://www.thefreelibrary.com/-a0186224296.

3. Stephanie Modkins, "Pastor of the Largest Church in the World Visits the Northwest," associatedcontent.com, March 26, 2008, http:// www.associatedcontent.com/article/679331/pastor_of_the_largest_ church_in_the.html.

4. http://www.youtube.com/watch?v=UIDLIwlzkgY.

ABOUT THE AUTHOR

D r. Myles Munroe is an international motivational speaker, best-
selling author, educator, leadership mentor, and consultant for government and business. Traveling extensively throughout the world, Dr.
Munroe addresses critical issues affecting the full range of human, social,
and spiritual development. The central theme of his message is the maxi-
mization of individual potential, including the transformation of followers
into leaders and leaders into agents of change.

Dr. Munroe is founder and president of Bahamas Faith Ministries
International (BFMI), a multidimensional organization headquartered in
Nassau, Bahamas. He is chief executive officer and chairman of the board
of the International Third World Leaders Association and president of the
International Leadership Training Institute.

Dr. Munroe is also the founder and executive producer of a number of
radio and television programs aired worldwide. In addition, he is a frequent
guest on other television and radio programs and international networks
and is a contributing writer for various Bible editions, journals, magazines,
and newsletters. He is a popular author of more than forty books, including *Becoming a Leader, The Most Important Person on Earth, The Spirit of
Leadership, The Principles and Power of Vision, Understanding the Purpose
and Power of Prayer, Understanding the Purpose and Power of Woman,* and
Understanding the Purpose and Power of Men.

For more than thirty years, Dr. Munroe has trained tens of thousands
of leaders in business, industry, education, government, and religion. He
personally addresses over 500,000 people each year on personal and professional development. His appeal and message transcend age, race, culture, creed, and economic background.

Dr. Munroe has earned B.A. and M.A. degrees from Oral Roberts
University and the University of Tulsa, and he has been awarded a number
of honorary doctoral degrees. He has also served as an adjunct professor of
the Graduate School of Theology at Oral Roberts University.

049357867

CHASE BRANCH LIBRARY
17731 W. SEVEN MILE RD.
DETROIT, MI 48235
578-8002